To Barbara,

with love

Liturgy
Made
Simple

Mark Searle

THE LITURGICAL PRESS   Collegeville, Minnesota

Nihil obstat: Joseph C. Kremer, S.T.L., *Censor deputatus.*

Imprimatur: ✝George H. Speltz, D.D., Bishop of St. Cloud, Minnesota, February 18, 1981.

Printed in the United States of America.

Cover design by Placid Stuckenschneider, O.S.B.

Third Printing, 1982

Library of Congress Cataloging in Publication Data

Searle, Mark   1941–
    Liturgy made simple.

    1. Catholic Church — Liturgy.   I. Title.
BX1970.S36   264'.02   81-4807
ISBN 0-8146-1221-0 (pbk.)   AACR2

Contents

Introduction

A favorite story that the English like to tell against themselves concerns two very proper gentlemen who found themselves marooned upon a desert island. For twenty years they survived upon that barren acreage, eating boiled eggs for breakfast, taking tea each afternoon, and all the while scanning the horizon, hoping to attract the attention of a passing ship. Yet, in all that time, so the story goes, they never once spoke to each other, inhibited by the fact that there was no one there to introduce them.

This little book needs no introduction, for it is itself an introduction. Curiously enough, there are many Catholics who have lived with the liturgy for a lifetime and yet have never really been introduced to it, with the result that they have never befriended it and come to know it. It has always been there, of course, but it has never really spoken to them. It has always seemed somewhat remote and unapproachable and beyond their comprehension. In the old days, that did not seem to matter very much. It was the priest's business, and the laity never thought of themselves as being more than reverent, silent on-lookers, keeping their distance and saying their own prayers. Then came Vatican II. Laypeople, as often as not, were dragged into the conversation, feeling as uncomfortable and ill-at-ease as the proverbial Englishman who finds himself addressed by a complete stranger.

This book is designed to "break the ice." It originated as four talks given at the Notre Dame Center for Pastoral Liturgy, talks designed for parishioners who found themselves called upon to take an active role in the planning and celebration of parish worship, but who felt that they did not really understand what it was all about. In their printed form they may serve much the same end and reach out to all who are trying to make sense of the liturgy we celebrate. Discussion questions have been appended to each chapter, with a view to encouraging the exploration of Christian liturgy in liturgy committees and other discussion groups.

An introduction is only the beginning of a new relationship. It is to be hoped that the reader will be led to move beyond this book to the celebration of the liturgy, and beyond a preoccupation with liturgical planning and performance to a deeper life lived within the mysteries we celebrate.

Liturgy Made Simple

DISCUSSION QUESTIONS

For use prior to reading the first chapter

1. When you think of "the Church," what images come to mind?

2. In the light of each image, what do you consider the purpose of the Church to be?

3. How do you see the liturgy and sacraments of the Church fitting into your images of the Church and your understanding of its purpose?

4. How does this view — or these differing views — of the liturgy affect (a) the way it is celebrated; (b) the question of who should be admitted to the sacraments?

1   *What Is Liturgy?*

Before discussing the details of specific rites, it might be helpful to establish a coherent picture of the liturgy of the Church. We hardly need to be told what the liturgy is, because we already know. It is rather like the man who was asked whether he believed in infant baptism. "No," he answered, "I've seen it." But the problem is this: when he saw baptism, what did he see? There is an old and familiar story about four blind men who were introduced to an elephant. Later, as they discussed their experience, they violently disagreed about what they had encountered. An elephant, claimed the first man, who had put his arms around the elephant's leg, is a kind of tree: a very large kind of tree is what an elephant is. No, argued the second man, an elephant is a kind of snake with a very coarse skin and a strange, soft mouth. He had, of course, grasped the elephant's trunk. The third man had felt the elephant's ear and swore black and blue that an elephant was a sail on a ship. The fourth man, who had grabbed the elephant's tail, was utterly convinced that an elephant was a piece of old rope.

I. Divergence of Views

Similarly, people have very different and often quite conflicting views on liturgy. This makes the celebration of the liturgy somewhat problematic. Mention the word "Mass" and some people think of quiet moments in a dark church with the priest afar off quietly muttering the words of ancient Latin and moving gently through the rote of time-hallowed ritual. Others think of guitars and joyful noises, of exuberance and movement and banners and enthusiastic congregations. Others think of a small gathering of friends and neighbors in someone's home for a careful reading of the Scriptures, for spontaneous prayer, and for intimate sharing of the one bread and the one cup. Others think of the Mass in terms of solemn ritual and beautiful music, a liturgy of pomp and circumstance, speaking of a concern to put the best of human gifts and talents at the service of worshipping the transcendent God. For others still, Mass is something you have to attend if you are a Catholic: just that and no more.

Obviously, all of these different views of the Mass lead to different ideas and expectations about what should and should not be. The same is true, of course, for the four men who met the elephant: it would be unwise to put any one of them in charge of the elephant house! The problem with the liturgy, however, is not that we are blind, or that any of these images of the Mass is entirely wrong. The problem is that the liturgy, like the Church itself, is a living mystery. That is, the liturgy, like the Church, is always more than we can say, and it eludes any easy definition. Yet most of us, on the basis of our experience or religious training, have a sort of working definition or an operational image in terms of which we naturally tend to judge liturgies as good or bad, agreeable or disagreeable.

The same is, of course, true of the Church: we all have our working definitions and we respond accordingly. The

National Catholic Reporter has a different image of Church than does *The Wanderer.* Dutch theologians – or some of them – have a different idea of what the Church is, and thus ought to be, than does the Pope. Different images of the Church create different sets of expectations and different ways of evaluating developments in the Church, whether the issue be the ordination of women or the Church's involvement in politics or the direction of ecumenism.

These kinds of disputes are not limited to the national and international scene; they percolate down into the parishes, creating tension and conflict. And it is in the parish that the liturgy is celebrated. Laws may be made in Rome, books may be written in Europe, directives may be issued from Washington, talks may be given at Notre Dame, but it is in a particular parish on a Sunday morning that out of all these rubrics and directives and bright ideas a community has to come to common worship, finding itself gathered together in the Spirit of Jesus before the presence of the Father. There the arguments have to cease – or at least be suspended – and common prayer has to rise up before the throne of God. Decisions have to be made on how we can all celebrate together, and this implies some basic common understanding of what it is we are all about. Celebrating *this* liturgy requires some consensus on what liturgy is for and what it means to be Church.

In this chapter, therefore, I will sketch the broad lines of an understanding of Church and liturgy which might help make sense of the liturgy and offer some sense of direction in its planning. It must be remembered, however, that we are dealing with a mystery when we are engaged with the Church and her liturgy. We are dealing with something which can never be completely understood or adequately defined, for it is always open to fresh insight and deeper understanding. I offer this sketch, then, not because it is *the* right one and all others are wrong, but simply to serve as a point of common reference for discussion. Much more needs to be said, but this can serve as a starting point: one that is as true as I can make it to the vision of Church and liturgy given to us in the Second Vatican Council.

II. THE CHURCH

One of the major considerations which prompted Pope John XXIII to summon the bishops of the world to Rome for the Council was the realization that the developments of modern history had led to a profound change of awareness about the Church and the world. We were in a new situation which raised new pastoral and theological questions. This situation had to be appraised and we had to look to our Tradition for fresh sources in responding to it.

Perhaps this new awareness of the Church's situation in the world can be most dramatically summarized in the use of an image.[1] If the whole history of humanity were scaled down to eight hours, the two thousand years of the Church's history would be represented by only the last couple of minutes. For most of its history, the human race has lived without the presence of the Church and its gospel in its midst. Moreover, even in the time that the Church

1. Juan Segundo, *The Community Called Church*, trans. John Drury, A Theology for Artisans of a New Humanity Series, vol. 1 (Maryknoll, N.Y.: Orbis Books, 1973).

has existed, it has never represented the religion of the majority of the human race. This has never really struck home until this century. Previously, Christians believed the world to be more or less evangelized. Of course, in the world as they saw it, there were always some who had still to be converted: underdeveloped peoples on the fringes of the world and a few recusant Jews in the midst of Christendom. But this was the world as they saw it; they were either ignorant of, or blind to, the existence of whole races and cultures living outside that world — peoples they had hardly discovered, living in the Americas and the Far East, in northern wastes and in the antipodes. Only in this century have we really come to full, global awareness of the extent and diversity of the human family. Only in this century have we come to realize, with something of a sense of shock, that most people on this earth have never been members of the Church and that even today, when Christianity is the most populous religion, its adherents still represent a minority of the human race.

This realization leads us to a more humble estimate of the success of Christianity and its role in history. It forces us to question the truth of our assertion that without faith and baptism no one can be saved.[2] Either God's plan was somewhat wider than we had imagined it, or else it was rather late coming into effect, or not very successful in its implementation. The small percentage of Christians in the world raises all sorts of questions, not only about how the unbaptized can be saved outside the Church, but about the

---

2. For a thoroughly researched, theological study of this question, *see* Jerome Theisen, *The Ultimate Church and the Promise of Salvation* (Collegeville, Minn.: St. John's University Press, 1976).

Church itself. If people can be saved outside the Church, i.e., if God can bring them to life with himself without the waters of baptism, then what is the Church for? If the Church is not absolutely necessary for salvation, what is it for at all?

Such questions have been debated by theologians and lay behind much of the discussion at Vatican II, but they have many ramifications in parish life as well. What is a parish for? Do we have to give the sacraments to anyone and everyone who shows up? Should we baptize every baby that comes our way, regardless of whether that child has any chance of being brought up as a believer? What attitude should we adopt towards people outside the Church?

This new self-realization of the Church's place in human history has led to a new self-image for the Church. Instead of thinking of itself as the only gateway to God, it has come increasingly to see itself as a sign established by God among the nations of the earth: a sign set up in history to show what God has done and is doing for the whole human race, whether he does it visibly or hiddenly.

What is this work of God in human history? It can perhaps best be summed up in the word "reconciliation." God is reconciling the world to himself by overcoming whatever is not of God. God is healing divisions, establishing justice where injustice rules, giving hope to the hopeless, light to the confused, peace to those who are at odds, and support to those whom hurt and fear have turned in upon themselves. In short, the work of God is his victory over sin and the establishment of his rule and Kingdom when evil would enslave us.

This new order is coming about, not only in individual

hearts, but in the human community itself. Thus, through the action of the Holy Spirit, the Kingdom — or rule — of God can spring up at any time and in any place: in a Chinese commune, an Indian village, a Russian factory, a Jewish kibbutz, an Arab family, an inner-city ghetto — wherever, and however fitfully, God's gracious and healing presence overcomes the power of evil. When the mistrust of neighbors is overcome in friendship, when an addict is helped to escape addiction, when a stranger finds welcome, when a person refuses to spread malicious gossip, when a mother by her unconditional love helps her child grow more self-confident and generous, when a nation takes a risk for peace — whenever such things happen there is the presence of God's Spirit, the power of his salvation, and the blossoming of his Kingdom.

The Church is to be a sign to the world of the work of God: not a signpost pointing somewhere else, but a sign, a manifestation, of what God is doing here for all. The Church is a community of people called to recognize and cooperate with that work of God. The Church is a community of believers whose faith is expressed in the acknowledgement of praise and prayer as well as in the acknowledgement that is expressed by putting one's life at the service of the Kingdom of God for the salvation of one's neighbors. The Church, therefore, is a community of people who are caught up wittingly and willingly in a continuing dynamic process: that of recognizing God's saving initiative (which we call "salvation" and "grace"), and that of responding to God himself and to his work. Thus there is, as it were, a double direction to this dynamic process: that of God's coming to us and that of our cooperative response to God.

This pattern of divine initiative and human response is precisely what we discern in the person, life, and actions of Jesus of Nazareth. We acknowledge him as "true God and true man." As "true God" he is the visible outreach of God to his human family, and as "true man" he is not only the visible revelation of God but also the very paradigm or model of human responsiveness to God. This in turn comes to characterize the life of the Church: the same pattern of divine initiative and human response which is manifest in the life and death of Jesus becomes the pattern by which the Church lives. (Even more than that, I would add that it is the underlying pattern of all human life and history insofar as they are true to their vocation as human beings.) In the life of the Church, therefore, just as in the life of Jesus, this twofold pattern of God's initiative and our response is meant to become visible. In ordinary human life it often passes unrecognized and unacknowledged, as we overlook and fail to see the heroism of the everyday. But God has brought it to visibility in the life of Jesus, and he calls for the Church, too, to embody it from generation to generation, precisely so that people may recognize that same pattern in their own lives and commit themselves to it — to the gracious presence of God and to the recognition and obedience which that presence entails. Consequently, it is impossible to overestimate, for the well-being of the *world*, the importance of faith and holiness in the *Church*. The Church cannot regard herself as simply "having the goods" ready to hand out, as if salvation were some kind of supernatural commodity. On the contrary, she is to be a sign of redemption in a world in process of being redeemed. But the world is being redeemed from the evil which prevents it from becoming what God intends it to be, and so the Church is supposed to be a sign of hope, a sign of what can be, a promise of a better world. Even here, however, we have no room to boast, for the Church is made up of people like us; it is part of the world and is itself in continual need of God's redemptive grace and of conversion and reform in response to that grace.

III.   THE LITURGY

In that broader context we can begin to appreciate the liturgy of the Church. The liturgy is really nothing else than the celebration of that ongoing process of redemption in and of the world. The liturgy is the "source and summit" of Christian life, as Vatican II called it, because it is in the liturgical celebration that that same pattern of initiative and response, of divine action and human cooperation, which underlies all Christian life and faith, comes to its most explicit expression.

This pattern and process of divine initiative and human response finds expression in the liturgy in various ways. The pattern of God's gracious initiative, his outreach towards us, is obviously expressed in the reading of his Word and in the gift of himself which comes to us through the various sacraments. But the first and basic sign of his intervention in human affairs is the very existence of the gathered congregation. If Catholics were asked why they attend Mass on any given Sunday, most would probably say they were there because it means a lot to them, or because they like worshipping in this parish, or because as Catholics they feel obliged to be there. Yet, if we reflect on it, we have to say that the reason people gather for Mass

on Sunday is that God has called them together. In contemporary society, where people believe all sorts of things
or don't believe at all, the faith that draws us to church on
Sunday, while one neighbor mows the lawn and another
sits and reads the papers, can give us a vivid sense of vocation or calling. It is not that we are better or worse than
our neighbors but that we, for God's own mysterious
reasons, have been selected and called by him to
acknowledge him and recognize what he is doing. The
Sunday congregation, however lukewarm and listless,
however confused and prejudiced it might be, is nevertheless what we refer to when we praise God on the grounds
that "from age to age you gather a people to yourself."

This congregation is the sign set among the nations — or
at least, set up in this neighborhood — to testify to the reality of God and to his concern for the human race. Of
course, it might not be a very good sign of God's salvation:
it can be riddled with cliques, smug and self-satisfied, lack-
ing any sense of itself as a Christian community, even rife
with prejudice and soiled with social injustice. Such a community hardly deserves the name of "Christian community" at all, for to the degree its life is shaped by the
ways of the world and not the ways of God it fails in its
vocation to be a sign.

That is one good reason why we have liturgy and why,
at the very beginning of the liturgy, we have a penitential
rite. The purpose of the penitential rite at the beginning of
the Mass is not so much to enable us to clean the slate of
personal peccadilloes but to enable us to recognize that,
although we have gathered to make visible the Body of
Christ, which is the Church, we have not lived as members
of that Body. We have not been faithful to our common

vocation to offer to the world a sign of hope and renewal;
we have not lived a lifestyle which contradicts the individualism, self-interest, and consumerism of the age; we
have not shown, together, that divisions, prejudice, injustice, and indifference can be overcome through the
power of God. Instead we have developed the kind of
spotty lives which enable us to merge unnoticed, like the
chameleon, into our secular environment. Thus God re-
mains unnoticed, unanswered and, indeed, helpless in the
world which belongs to him but does not know him.

Still, even recognizing our common and personal infidelity, when we gather together for the celebration of the
liturgy, that is what we are: a people called together by
God to be his witnesses and his fellow-workers in human
history. We are the Body of Christ, his arms and legs and
feet and hands, for the world he loves. The liturgy, says
Pope Pius XII, is the worship of the whole Body of Christ,
head and members. At the liturgy, we are summoned together into the presence of the Father, who is the Father of
all. We are gathered "in Christ," for without Christ we
could not so stand before God. And we are gathered
through the Spirit of Christ, who is poured out into our
hearts to form us into "one body, one spirit, in Christ."

Thus the coming together of the congregation is a sign
and symbol of what God is doing and where his work is
going. God's work in history, we have seen, is to gather
into one the scattered children of God, to overcome
divisions, to provide a place for the homeless and the
lonely, to give support to those whose burdens are heavy,
and to create an oasis of community in the midst of a
world painfully divided into the haves and the have-nots.
Here, in the congregation of God, we are all to discover

our common humanity and to set aside our inequities. The gathering of believers is meant to be the anticipation of the day when God's Kingdom will be established in all its fullness, when there will be no more discrimination on the grounds of sex, race, or wealth; when there will be no more hunger and thirst, no more mistrust and mutual violence, no more competitiveness and abuse of power, for all things will be subject to Christ, and God will reign over his people in peace and for ever. In the words of Vatican II:

> The liturgy daily builds up those who are in the Church, making of them a holy temple of the Lord, a dwelling-place for God in the Spirit, to the mature measure of the fullness of Christ. At the same time it marvelously increases their power to preach Christ and thus show forth the Church, a sign lifted up among the nations . . . under which the scattered children of God may be gathered together until there is one fold and one shepherd. (*Constitution on the Sacred Liturgy*, 2)

IV. LITURGICAL CHANGES

That sounds fine in theory or as an ideal, but it was precisely to make that ideal both more credible and more realizable that Vatican II undertook the reform of the liturgy. The problem with the liturgy is that, like all enterprises involving human beings, it can get tired and stale and settle into a rut, or it can even be put to uses for which it was not intended. For example, the liturgy was from the beginning a community affair, but in the course of time it became more or less privatized. I mean not only "private Masses," but "private baptism," "private penance," and the whole way of celebrating which relied upon the activity of an authorized priest and the more or less passive presence of a congregation that was more a collection of individuals than an organic unity. As a result, the liturgy was seen as being primarily for the sanctification of individuals who were baptized, confirmed, or went to Mass for the benefit of their own interior lives. Even at Sunday Mass, the community event par excellence, people were scattered about the church engaging in their private prayers and devotions as the Mass went on at the altar.

The rubrics of the Old Mass, as they were fixed in the sixteenth century, were exclusively concerned with the priest. They began with the words: "When the priest is duly vested, he takes the chalice in his left hand . . . and carries it in front of him, his right hand resting on the burse which is placed on top of the chalice; and, making a reverence to the Cross, or to an image thereof, in the sacristy, he proceeds to the altar with his head covered and with the server going before him with the Missal and whatever else might be necessary. . . ." The new equivalent of that rubric reads, "When the people have assembled, the priest and ministers proceed to the altar in the following order. . . ." Moreover, the old rubrics mentioned the congregation only three times: once to indicate the direction in which the priest should say "Dominus vobiscum"; once to suggest that, after the priest has received Communion from the chalice, "if there are some who wish to communicate," he may give Communion; and finally, to tell the priest to face the people when giving the blessing. In the *General Instruction on the Roman Missal* (1969) the Order of Mass with a Congregation is made normative, and much is made of the role of the people as a whole and of the various ministries within the assembly.

Nevertheless, if in the past the liturgy became something highly formal and individualistic, the danger today is perhaps that it often risks becoming a sort of churchy hoe-down. In reaction against the timelessness and other-worldliness of the old liturgy, and in the quest for what is often referred to as "meaningful" and "relevant," some groups turn liturgical celebrations into affirmations of life and faith which are often too flimsy and too superficial to be sustaining. Many parishes have found that the youth Masses which attracted such enthusiasm a few years ago are now becoming stereotyped and boring and that the music and lyrics collected in the now worn-out parochial anthologies have come to sound banal.

A poster in a convent chapel proclaims: "Celebrate life where you find it!"—a sentiment not untypical of the liturgies of the last fifteen years. But the problem is, where is life found? Is this living? Faith and liturgy which are content to affirm the goodness of everything and which harp on the theme of joy, joy, joy are not true to life as we know it nor to the Christian tradition. Whereas the old liturgy tended to lock each of us into our own private devotional world, the new liturgy can be celebrated in such a way that we end up being locked into pseudo-togetherness. The painful and challenging experiences of life are simply ignored, and we pretend the Kingdom is already here or at least just waiting to be ushered in with waves and cheers.

The problem with both these approaches to liturgy is that they collapse the tension which is inherent in Christian living and in the liturgy itself. The first, with its emphasis on the supernatural, the private, and the otherworldly, looks to a future which has nothing intrinsically to do with life on earth. Life on earth is just an obstacle course for pious souls; the Kingdom of God will be their reward in the hereafter. This view also tends to see God in his heaven and the devil in the world, so that the sacraments are means of getting grace to join the one and fight the other — but all very interiorly and privately.

The other, more contemporary view emphasizes the reality of Christ's presence in the world: in sunsets and butterflies and human faces. It talks a lot about community and togetherness and love as present realities. The world is good and people are good and life is good and we are good and God is good: "Go tell everyone the news that the Kingdom is come!" Bum-bum! This view tends to see God everywhere and the devil nowhere, and the sacraments are all "celebrations," which means they ought to be fun.

V. Tensions in Christian Life and Liturgy

Admittedly, these two views of liturgy are caricatures, and the adherents of either view could justifiably complain. I offer these caricatures, however, not so much to mock people's devotion as to call to our awareness the tension that has to be retained. And the word is tension, not balance. Tension creates energy; balance, once achieved, presumes a state of repose. No, there needs to be in our liturgy a tension between the present and the future, between the personal and the communal, between the ideal of the Kingdom and the realities of present experience in the world. In the life of Jesus, it was this tension which was the message of his preaching and work: "The Kingdom is here, in your midst; therefore repent!" (Not "have fun!") But even here where the Kingdom is, there is still a world where the Kingdom is not yet in control. We have no doubt of the outcome, but this confidence is a call to obedience and mission, not an excuse to play around. The work of God is in process: this means that we still need his redemption, as individuals, as communities, as nations, as a race. It means that we are not alone and that we need never despair, but it also means that we are called to work for that Kingdom, to allow God to be king, to rule in our hearts and in our society. Either to act as if all were accomplished and all were well with the world, or else to act as if the world and its affairs had nothing to do with a Kingdom that will only be established after death and out of time, would be to misunderstand both the nature of Christian life and the nature of Christian liturgy.

The liturgy is of the present, but it points to the future. It is of this world, but it points to a reality which transcends present experience. It is of the present, because it celebrates and makes real the presence among us of the God who is saving the world in Christ, but that very presence makes us painfully aware of how far we are from the Kingdom of God. It constitutes a call to live and work for the values of God, which are not the values of a society which takes for granted inequality, competitiveness, prejudice, infidelity, international tension, and unbounded consumption. The liturgy celebrates the presence of God's Kingdom, but it is a presence which contradicts us in many ways and calls us into a future that is of God's making and not a construct of Western civilization. Thus it continually challenges us to repent, to be converted, to live a new and different kind of life.

Likewise, the liturgy is of this world, yet it points to a way of being in the world which recognizes its real depth of meaning. For example, liturgy draws on all the elements of our lives: our bodies, significant persons, society, and the things we use to sustain and enhance our lives. It teaches us to use our bodies to house the presence of God, to worship him and to serve him, and to bring his Word and healing to others. It teaches us to listen to the voice of God in the voice of others, and to receive at the hands of others the gifts of God himself. It teaches us to live in the society of others, people of different background and different race, as men and women committed to peace and unity and mutual help. It teaches us to use the goods of the earth — represented in the liturgy by bread and wine and water and oil — not as goods to be grabbed, accumulated, and consumed, but as sacraments of the Creator himself, to be accepted with thanksgiving, handled with reverence, and shared with generosity.

Yes, the liturgy *is* an expression of our faith and love, but it also shapes and deepens our faith and love. It teaches us how to live with faith and how to come to deeper and truer love. It teaches us that faith, hope, and love come to life to the degree that we acknowledge and surrender to the work of God in the world. The liturgy, we know, begins and ends with the Sign of the Cross, for it is the Cross which is the sign both of God's love for us and of Jesus' human response to that love. He loved to the end, he was obedient even to death on a Cross.

Thus the liturgy brings us to the realization that there is no love without sacrifice, no life except through death to "life as we know it." In the liturgy and in life we identify ourselves with the death of Jesus, so that the life of Jesus, too, may become manifest in us. The heart of the liturgy, the heart of all the sacraments, from baptism to the rites for the dying, is the paschal mystery: the mystery of God's initiative and our response as revealed in the death and resurrection of the Lord.

So we come back to where we began, to the role of the Christian community in the world. The reason why there is a community of believers is to acknowledge the work of God in human life and to cooperate with the purposes of God in human history. That work is a work of love and redemption, involving submission to God and commitment to the renewal of the face of the earth. It is not only bread and wine which are transformed in the liturgy; *we* are to be transformed by associating ourselves in the self-sacrifice of Jesus, that God may raise us up continually to newness of life. But it does not end there, for the bread and wine are transformed so that we might be transformed, and we are transformed so that the Church might be transformed, and the Church is to be transformed continually so that the world itself might be transformed by being rebuilt under the rule of God for the well-being of all humanity.

The liturgy is not the be-all and end-all of the Christian life; Vatican II speaks of it only as the "source and summit" of Christian living, admitting that there are many other things to be done in between. Nevertheless, we can learn from the liturgy the pattern of God's presence in the world, discerning his saving presence in all human situations in the light of his more explicit presence in the language and symbols of the liturgy. The liturgy makes explicit what is hidden and implicit in human history: it recalls what God has done in the past, that we might recognize the same God at work in the present, and it reminds us of the goal to which the world and its history are to be directed. It puts us in touch with the mystery that lies at the very heart of things.

VI. CONCLUSION: SOME GENERAL PRINCIPLES

This sketchy presentation of a theology of the liturgy is not going to provide easy answers for all practical questions about what must be done, whether in planning a liturgy or in living our lives. It is intended simply to serve as a basis for reflection and discussion of what we are about when we are planning and celebrating liturgies, and to offer a view of the wider context within which such planning takes place. For as we all know too well, we can get so preoccupied with the details that we lose sight of the whole and find ourselves proposing liturgical changes without much sense of the larger shape of things. In conclusion, a few general principles might be useful.

1. Liturgy is never perfect. The liturgy we celebrate will never be adequate to the mystery it contains. More often than not, our liturgical celebrations will speak not only of the wonders of God, but of the brokenness and limitations of us who celebrate. Too easily we get caught in a critical attitude and then become angry and frustrated at the stupidity of our brothers and sisters in Christ, even to the point where we can no longer give ourselves over to the prayer of the liturgy. The only way out of that is to allow the Spirit of God to convert our indignation into compassion. This does not mean giving up the effort to improve our liturgical celebrations, but it does mean recognizing that at the heart of our liturgy stands the one who emptied himself for our sakes, the one who had compas-

sion on the multitude, the one who was treated as a fool and put to death by those who were exasperated by him.

2. Liturgy does not always have to be different. The temptation of all liturgy planners is to look for new and exciting ways of doing things. But liturgy is ritual, not entertainment. It is meant to form us, not to have us on the edge of our seats. The liturgy keeps bringing us back to old *words* until we begin to understand them, and to old *signs* until we begin to see what they mean. Our care should be to let the words be heard, to let the images shimmer, to let the gestures be done so clearly that they speak for themselves. A corollary of this is that liturgical texts and actions should not be continually explained; they are rich in meaning, inviting insight, not explanation.

3. Liturgy is prayer. It involves prayerful togetherness, prayerful hearing of the Word, prayerful concern for the larger world, prayerful acknowledgement of the works of God, prayerful acceptance of the gifts of God, and prayerful acceptance of his commission to go and serve his Kingdom in our lives. The place where the community gathers, wherever that may be, is not a classroom or a dance hall or a theater or a cafeteria or a private meditation room; it is a house of common prayer for the People of God.

4. Liturgy is not so much a celebration of life-as-we-know-it as it is a celebration of the mystery of life we hardly suspect. While it uses the stuff of everyday life — word and song, movement and food, meeting and touching, candles and flowers, tables and chairs — it uses them all with a sense of the holiness of these things. This holiness

is derived not so much from their presence in a sacred place as from a recognition of the sacred presence which pervades all places. The people and language and things of the liturgy are to be handled with reverence and care. Ours is a pragmatic culture, with little sense of the lovely. Part of our liturgical ministry will be to ensure that the things we use and the things we do liturgically serve to develop people's sensitivity to the loveliness of all created things, a loveliness which is but an expression and reflection of the beauty of the Creator himself.

5. Liturgy is "service" — an ambiguous term referring both to our service of God and to God's service of us. Both senses of the term come together in our service of one another, for it is God who serves and is served in the mutual care we show one another. Sometimes, when we are exercising a liturgical ministry — whether it be reading or playing music or acting as an usher or a minister of Communion — we find ourselves "distracted." Maybe so. But it is also important for us to be aware of who it is we serve when we serve one another, or else our ministry itself may become distracting to others.

DISCUSSION QUESTIONS

1. Do you find your image(s) of the Church strengthened or challenged?

2. Do you find the images of the Church offered in this chapter more or less helpful in understanding what the Church is for? What practical differences does a change of image make?

3. Is your understanding of the liturgy confirmed, altered or radically challenged in this reading? What practical difference does it make for you?

4. What has been the experience of the group in discussing these topics and reading this chapter?

5. Has any common understanding emerged, and what differences remain? Are the differences such as to lead to different decisions about liturgical practice?

2 The Liturgy of the Word

One sign that a person is familiar with a particular piece of machinery or is a competent architect or may be trusted to do a surgical operation is that one knows "which end is up," which piece fits into which, and the general principles of how the machine or the building or the body functions. So it is with liturgy. Just as we would not want one of the four blind men mentioned earlier put in charge of training elephants for the circus, so it can be disastrous to commit the task of liturgical planning to people whose interests, education, and gifts lie elsewhere. For example, the ability to play the organ does not thereby qualify someone to choose the hymns without further ado, and a simple desire to be of service to the parish community does not automatically qualify a person to design and manufacture liturgical banners. The musician and the banner-maker both have their parts to play, but they also both need an overall sense of what the liturgical celebration is about and how all its parts fit together.

Before plunging into a consideration of the Liturgy of the Word, then, it seems worthwhile to pause briefly for a look at the overall pattern of the liturgy. Although our main concern is the Mass, we may note that the basic shape and structure of all sacramental celebrations are much the same. What we say here about Eucharist, therefore, can easily be applied to baptism, penance, and so on.

There are basically four parts to the Mass: four parts which have their equivalent in the other sacramental liturgies. The two main parts are the Liturgy of the Word and the Liturgy of the Eucharist or sacrament. These represent the main items on the agenda: first talk, then action. The celebration, however, does not plunge immediately into dialogue with God. It begins rather more slowly, trying to create the right atmosphere through the Introductory Rites. Likewise, the community does not just break up as soon as people have been fed. There is time for community announcements and so forth before the dismissal of the people. So there are four parts: Introductory Rites, Liturgy of the Word, Liturgy of the Eucharist, Concluding Rites. It is important, especially for liturgy planners and ministers, to understand three things: [1] how the overall shape of the liturgy makes sense; [2] how each part fits into the whole in terms of its meaning; and [3] how each part contributes to the sense of the next. The liturgy is rather like a symphony in four movements, where the whole thing holds together as each part is given its proper place and value in relation to the whole. So when we look at the four parts of the Mass, we want to keep an eye on how each part fits with the rest.

The main topic of this chapter is the Liturgy of the Word, but it makes sense to begin with the Introductory Rites preceding it. This is obviously to proceed in the order in which the liturgy of the Mass unfolds: first Introductory Rites, then Liturgy of the Word. But as we shall see, when we come to planning we work in the reverse order: we start with the readings and then work back to the Introductory Rites. This is because one of the major responsibilities of any liturgical planning group is to make sure that the Introductory Rites are set up in such a way that people are really ready, by the end of them, to hear the Word of God.

I. INTRODUCTORY RITES

In the liturgy, as in many other instances, it is important to get off on the proper foot, because if we bungle the start it is hard to make it up later. We know what it is like when we compare experiences of different liturgies. In one church, we are strangers in a crowd, the people are scattered listlessly around the church, there is no music, the celebrant shuffles to the altar and starts off, "In the name of the Father . . . let us call to mind our sins," while still hunting for his place in the missal and looking as though he has still not noticed whether there is anyone out there to respond or not. In another church, we sense there is something afoot when we step inside the door. People obviously know each other and are preparing to celebrate together. The way things are set up gives us a hint that they know what they are celebrating. This is confirmed when the opening music and the opening remarks of the celebrant have something to do with one another and with what follows.

Once again, though, it is hard for the beginner to make much sense of the Introductory Rites: entrance hymn or antiphon, reverencing of the altar, Sign of the Cross, greeting of the people, introductory remarks, call to penance, penitential rite (3 forms to choose from!), *Kyries, Gloria* (sometimes!), and finally the collect. Now that is a lot of bits and pieces, and it is obvious that in many churches people haven't got the hang of it. The problem is not just theirs; it is in the rite itself, where the desire to keep as many traditional elements as possible overcame the initial desire to simplify the whole thing. For this reason, it is important to remember what the Introductory Rites are for: they are to prepare the people to take part in the Mass, i.e., to hear the Word of God, to pray, and to celebrate the Eucharist.

The only really indispensable part of the Introductory Rites is the collect or opening prayer. This is the point to which everything else leads, the point at which this crowd of people, who have just come from their homes or workplaces, or from shopping or partying or whatever, can find themselves together as a community. The idea is that, wherever we have come from, whatever we've been doing, we come together now as the Body of Christ. We lose our individuality to find our common identity; we let the noise and preoccupations of our lives die away as we become aware of him in whose presence we stand, and of those with whom we stand.

Thus the entrance hymn or other music must help us find our common identity, become aware of our standing in the presence of God in Christ, and be attentive to his Word. The penitential rite is placed at the beginning of Mass for this purpose. It provides for a moment of silent recollection — recollection of who we are and who we are called to be as members of the Body of Christ. It is not so much a moment for asking forgiveness for our personal sins as for asking God to forgive our failure to live together as a sign to the world, as the Body of Christ. This is the usual way of coming into the presence of God; but the *Gloria*, to be used on joyous occasions, presents an alternative. This ancient hymn, which is many centuries old, is an acclamation of God the Father and of his Christ, present among us who are members of his Body. The mood of the penitential rite and the mood of the *Gloria* are quite different, and it is hard to shift from the sobriety of the confession of sin to the exuberance of the *Gloria* without feeling forced. Generally speaking, it is better to choose either the penitential rite or the *Gloria*, rather than have both. Alternatively, we might use form three of the penance rite — the form that incorporates the *Kyries* — but use it as an acclamation of Christ: "You are the Son of the Living God; Lord, have mercy. You are the Savior of the world; Christ, have mercy. You are the joy of all who trust in you; Lord, have mercy." Then, omitting the absolution, we can go straight into the *Gloria* without much problem.

But the main purpose of the Introductory Rites is to form a worshipping community. Hence they lead up to the collect, the first solemn prayer offered in the name of the community to the Father, through and in the Son, by the power of the Holy Spirit. The second purpose is to prepare people to hear the Word of God by giving them a sense of occasion, a sense of expectancy, and a sense of what to listen for. This does not mean that they have to be given a synopsis of the readings in the priest's introductory remarks. Far better that some question be raised there about an area of our life to which the readings might subsequently speak. But let us at least have it clear in our minds what we are trying to do in arranging the Introductory Rites and keep everything subservient to that most important end: forming a praying community.

II. The Liturgy of the Word

If there is one thing that stands in the way of people
understanding the Mass, it is the feeling that the Mass consists of just one thing coming after another, with no ap-
parent rhyme or reason. We have already alluded to this
problem with regard to the Introductory Rites, but it is
equally if not more true with regard to the Liturgy of the
Word. If we had a completely free hand and could start
from scratch to design a Mass liturgy, would we determine
that there should be three readings plus a psalm (which
often becomes yet another reading), and that at least one
of those readings need have nothing to do with the other
two? Probably not. Would we, in fact, have readings from
Scripture at all? Why not have a selection from Hans
Küng, or Pope John Paul II, or some other stimulating contemporary writers? Why not just a film or a lecture on
some religious topic? Would that not be more useful?
These questions prompt the further questions of why have
a Liturgy of the Word and why read the Scriptures? Are
they important values?

Another way of putting this is to ask: what are we trying to do? Is the Liturgy of the Word meant to be a period
of religious instruction or edification? If so, perhaps
discussion groups, filmstrips, and other things would do
the job better. But the conclusion of each reading gives us a
clue. "This is the Word of the Lord," the reader says.
"Thanks be to God," we reply. This is the Word of the
Lord: not instruction about God, but the Word *of* God,
the Word addressed to us by God himself. Now that is different from religious instruction — and a lot of priests have
not yet learned the difference, for they turn their homilies

into moral diatribes or financial appeals or doctrinal instructions or scriptural exegesis instead of helping us hear the Word of God. They talk about God instead of letting God speak to us.

But how does God speak to us? What is this "Word of the Lord"? We usually assume that it is the scriptural message that has just been read: the actual text. But it is as well to remember that the traditions we find in our Bible today — whether ancient histories, songs, wisdom sayings, re-worked myths, or edifying stories — all came into existence as oral stories and were handed down as such. Even the Gospels in the New Testament are the later edited version of large collections of stories about the sayings and doings of Jesus. But even then, these stories are about something else: they are not stories about stories, but ultimately they are stories about things that happened or were said. Or they are reflections upon things that happened. So which is the Word of God: the texts we have in our books, or the stories that were handed down, or the events that the stories are about? Well, in a sense it is all three, but obviously the first two depend upon the third.

In the Hebrew language of the Old Testament, the term used for "word" (*dabar*) could also mean an event, especially an important or significant or meaningful event: an event that said something. There are even relics of this old usage in the New Testament. In the Douai version of the Gospel of Luke, for example, the shepherds, to whom the angels had appeared as they guarded their sheep in the hills near Bethlehem, say to one another, "Let us go to Bethlehem and *see this word* that has come to pass" (italics added). This reflects the way in which the term "Word of God" or "Word of the Lord" is best understood. God communicates to his people, not by putting thoughts into their heads or whispering into their ears, but by doing significant things in human lives. Thus the escape from Egypt was a very significant event for the Israelites. At the time they were probably scared out of their skins and had no thoughts but to put as much distance between themselves and the Egyptians as possible. Still, in retrospect, they began to realize that this was some significant event, some *dabar*. Of course, what it said to them was quite different from what the same event said to the Egyptians, for they recognized the saving intervention of the God they served.

Similarly, in Christian tradition we talk of Jesus as a *dabar:* he not only speaks in God's name, but he *is* the Word of God made flesh. His very person, present among the people of first-century Palestine, was a significant or meaningful event: a *dabar* or Word of God. The Scriptures, whether they be the Gospels or the epistles, are all derived more or less directly from the person of Jesus: who he was, what he did, how he died and how he had an impact on other people's lives. All that is the Word of God, and the New Testament writings in their own different ways record and reflect upon the person of Jesus and his life and death. Thus they are the Word of the Lord in a derived sense, for they are the record of events, not the events themselves.

This brings us to the second point about reading the Scriptures, which is that the Scriptures are the written memory of the Church. The Scriptures, as we have just seen, are the written record of and reflection on the acts of God in the past, whether it be in the Exodus or in Jesus. But of what use is that to us? Why should we remember the past? Why do we keep on telling these old stories? Has

God stopped working? Has he no more to say? Are there no longer any "significant events"?

Of course God still acts, and of course he still speaks, but how would we recognize him? If we are waiting for the thunder and lightning of theophany, we will probably be disappointed. God speaks in ways which can be easily overlooked. After all, the Egyptians overlooked the presence of God in the Exodus, and many contemporaries of Jesus thought he was a good man, but they were not expecting to experience him as God incarnate. So why should we expect that God will trumpet his presence for us? May it not be that he speaks in the events and circumstances of our own lives and times and we fail to recognize him? The problem may be not that God is absent or silent, but that we do not know his language.

To illustrate, let us imagine that we are foreigners in a strange, distant country. All around us we see boards with squiggles covering them. We suppose the markings are writing, but we cannot begin to decipher them. We hear people around us chattering away, but to us it is all noise — we do not even know where one word begins and another ends. The problem, of course, is that we have never heard or seen the local language before. And never having heard or seen it before, we do not recognize what all these people are saying or reading on the signs.

It is only on occasions like this, when communication breaks down, that we realize how dependent we are upon our memories even for ordinary, everyday things. Even in reading this page, we are using our memories — recognizing words we have seen and used before — thus we are able to make sense of the text. If we cannot remember coming across such words before, they are just meaningless marks on a page. The same is true of many other things: without memory we are lost. If suddenly we found that we had totally lost our memory, we would surely panic. We would not know who we were, how we had come to be here, what we were doing here, who all these other people were. In fact, if we had a complete loss of memory, we would be unable to speak or to understand what was being said to us. Without memory, we would not know what anything was about.

All this is simply by way of stressing how important memory is to us. The remembrance of the past is the key to understanding the present. If we want to understand the situation in Iran, we study the history of that area of the world. So, too, with other matters. That is why we read the Scriptures: because they are the memory of the Church. They are not read simply for their own sakes, as some old people keep living in the past, rehearsing their memories, hardly present to us at all. The Scriptures are not read as a book of rules, either, as if God spoke once in the past in a pre-industrial, pre-technological world and laid down the precise rules that people would have to live by even when they gave up looking after sheep and went to the moon instead. No, the Scriptures are read as the memory which makes the present intelligible, to help us understand our own lives and interpret the significant events in our lives and in our world as "Word of God."

In the circumstances of our own lives and our own time, then, the Word of God comes to us, but it can be recognized and understood and responded to only in the light of the memories of God's actions in the past. To know and understand other persons we have to know something of their history. Knowing others well means knowing something of their past, how they usually think and feel and act. If we don't know other persons well, we can easily misjudge and misunderstand them. So it is with God. Recalling his relationship with people in the past, and especially his presence and activity in the person of Jesus, we know something at least of the kind of God he is, and we continue to understand him better as we continue to live with him today. We come to understand what he is doing for us and what he is calling us to do.

That is why we read the Scriptures. That too is why in the revised Lectionary we have readings from the Old Testament as well as the Gospel. The Old Testament reading, followed by the New Testament reading, gives us a sense of perspective, a perspective which does not end with the Gospel but which runs from the past, through the present, and into the future. The Old Testament readings on Sundays and during the seasons of Advent, Lent, and Easter always have some connection with the Gospel. For example, on the Ninth Sunday in Ordinary Time (Year C), the Gospel tells of Jesus' cure of the centurion's servant. When we go back to the Old Testament reading, we find it is taken from the first book of Kings and is an excerpt from Solomon's prayer at the dedication of the Temple. Solomon prays God to hear the prayers even of non-Jews, of foreigners who come from a distant country. Thus the Gospel is in a sense God's response to the prayer of Solomon, for Jesus hears the petition of a Roman soldier, a non-Jew, and gives his servant life. This, in turn, prompts us to look at our own situation. How do we feel about foreigners? Who are the foreigners who come to our country today looking for life? The Cuban refugees, the boat people, the millions of people all over the globe who are

victims of violence, war, economic collapse, racial perse-
cution, and so forth. Maybe, like the centurion, they have
a faith in God which, while not our faith, nevertheless puts
us to shame. But will their faith and hope be in vain? Will
they be left to die, their prayers unanswered? Or will they
find God acting today, as in the past, through his chosen
ones? Are we being called by God, through the circumstances of our life and times, to cooperate with him in
welcoming the stranger, sheltering the homeless, raising up
the lowly?

On the Tenth Sunday in Ordinary Time (Year C), the
Gospel tells of Jesus giving life to the only son of a wid-
owed mother. The first reading tells of Elijah the prophet
doing the same, centuries before. So where does that leave
us? If God is a God who raises the dead and comforts the
bereaved, where do we find him in action today? We could
find many more examples, but the point is clear. In a very
real sense, the homily is meant to serve as a "contemporary
reading" in line with the Old Testament and the Gospel,
pointing to the signs of the times, the places and events in
which God's activity and Word can be seen and heard, inviting us to join him and become his co-workers and his
witnesses.

Frequently the second reading at Sunday Mass is difficult to "connect" with the other two. This is because it is
selected on a different principle. The Gospel passages are
taken more or less in sequence. The Old Testament reading
is selected to shed light on the Gospel. But the second
reading, usually from the epistles, is part of a continuous
reading of a particular book. Sometimes it does shed light
on the other two readings, but sometimes it is on a different track completely, and many people find this confus-

ing. It is hard to know what to do about this, but sometimes it might be better to omit it altogether. The rubrics permit this for "pastoral reasons," and I would think that the causing of confusion would be a good pastoral reason. Perhaps when that happens, the passage concerned could be printed in the parish bulletin, so that people could read it for themselves, either before Mass, or at home during the week.

If these reflections make sense, one can see that there are good reasons for keeping to the reading of the Scriptures and following the Lectionary — at least in theory. The question of how to present the readings in the liturgy, however, is a different matter. On this there are two things to say, the first involving preparation and the second execution.

On the question of preparation, it is essential that the liturgy planners, the celebrant, and the readers have done their homework. We plan a liturgy, prepare a sermon, and practice the readings so that people who come to church on a Sunday morning with no preparation can be helped in every way possible to hear and understand the Word of the Lord. This means that the celebrant and the planning committee, as well as the readers, have to read the Scripture texts and do a kind of shared meditation on them, anticipating the community's listening to those same readings on Sunday. What are the images given in the readings? With what aspects of our own life-experience do they link up? Also, to be sure that the Scripture passages are properly understood, they need to be put back in their original context. For example, the Sunday reading may offer a small excerpt from Solomon's prayer, but to appreciate what that means, we must see the whole prayer and the circumstances surrounding it. Similarly, the readings need to be read in association with one another and compared. There is little chance that the congregation will understand the Scripture passages if those responsible for the celebration and those doing the reading and preaching have not themselves understood the gist of the texts ahead of time. Thus readers have not simply to read a text aloud, but to proclaim the message contained in the text; so they must know the point of the story or the prayer or the psalm they are reading. If they do not know what it is about, there is little chance any of their hearers will.

Secondly, in terms of the actual execution of the readings, the goal is to ensure that people have every chance of hearing and understanding what is read. Communications theory tells us that a message consists not in what we intend to say but in what we are understood to say. So we can easily fail to communicate, unless we are genuinely concerned to communicate well. This means, in the first place, ensuring that people can actually hear the reader. Most of us who are involved in the liturgy usually find ourselves up at the front of the church, but the criterion of communication is what the people in the back can hear. A survey a few years ago showed that 70% of Americans going to Mass on Sunday couldn't hear what was being read or said in the sanctuary. Therefore, the amplifying system must be effective.

Sometimes, the concern to communicate is satisfied by the purchase of an expensive public address system; but there is more to it than that. People need to be prepared to hear: they need a word of introduction. We must use that term with caution because sometimes introductions to the readings are as long as the readings themselves! But if we enter a church on a Sunday morning and hear Solomon's prayer being read, or the story of Elijah curing some woman's sick child, we wonder what that has to do with us. Why is it being read? The kind of introduction we need is not so much one that gives Solomon's dates, or hints at the exegetical difficulties of the books of Kings, but one that provides a context for hearing this text today. For example, the introduction might usefully take the form of a question such as: "What are we to think about the arrival of so many Cubans in Florida? Can we simply judge the issue in terms of our own economic situation and the threat to our standard of living? Is that how God acts with us?" Or, for the widow of Naim and Elijah's cure of the young boy: "Any of you who have had contact with a hospital will be familiar with the incredible capabilities of modern medicine, but are good techniques enough? When you are sick or bereaved, is it efficiency you look for, or something more? What is it that makes human life so precious?" These introductory words need to be kept very short: in fact, it might be better if they were left out here and included in the celebrant's introductory and welcoming remarks. The point is to start people thinking, to give them something to listen for in the readings, something that can be taken up and elaborated in the homily. As the philosopher Alfred Whitehead remarked, "In the real world it is more important that a proposition be interesting than that it be true. The importance of truth is that it adds to interest." Too often we forget that. We juggle with truths which do not become true for us until they arouse our interest. So the introduction to the readings — and to the Mass — should be designed to arouse the interest of the worshippers, and the truth can take it from there.

But if something is interesting, we need a chance to reflect on it and to see whether it is true. In other words, we need to give people a chance to assimilate what they have heard, to think about it and even to begin to pray. Too often the Liturgy of the Word is words, words, words, and one thing after another. Let us have a little tranquility: readings read slowly enough for us to be able to ponder them, to allow us to be struck by a word or an image, and then a moment to live with it before going on to the next thing, whether it is a psalm or another reading. Sometimes it is a good idea to vary the psalm: perhaps have it sung as a solo, or perhaps replace it with music, or simply with silence. As often as not it is quite appropriate to have everyone join in the antiphon, but when it becomes totally routine and is always sung antiphonally it can become meaningless. A traffic signal which is always stuck on red and never changes to green is meaningless. We should introduce variety into our liturgies, not simply for variety's sake, but so that the choice of this reading or hymn or penitential rite, or this way of doing the psalm, can be seen to be meaningful. Variation can be very significant or it can be quite without significance. The flashing of different colored lights at an intersection, and the time for which each color shines, is very significant. The totally arbitrary changing of colors in the lights on a Christmas tree is nice, but meaningless. Again, the point is simply this: to ask how we can create optimum conditions under which people can hear and respond to the Word of the Lord.

Responses to the Word take us beyond the readings and the homily to the Creed and the intercessions. Both of these are in the liturgy because people have in the past found that what they wanted to do after taking the Word of God to heart was to give an assent of faith to what they had heard and to express their confidence in the God who had spoken to them, by commending to him the needs of the world. In fact, though, one should not overlook the fact that *the* response to the Word of God is the celebration of the sacrament which follows, whether that be baptism or marriage or Eucharist or whatever. As we shall see when we discuss the Eucharist, it really makes sense only as a response of faith and love to the Father, who has done and is doing such great things for us. Nevertheless, before we come to the Eucharist, we have the Creed and the intercessions, so a word about each.

The Creed is actually a transplant. It belongs, really, not at Mass but at baptism. In fact the Apostle's Creed is the old baptismal formula of Rome, and the Nicene Creed developed out of the baptismal formula used in the early centuries in the Christian community at Jerusalem. It owes its place in the Mass to the desire to respond to God's works, as proclaimed in the readings, by an affirmation of faith in all God has done, is doing, and will yet do. Often this is quite appropriate, though historically its use has been restricted to certain occasions. It is a pity we have to have it every Sunday. For one thing, not every set of readings would spontaneously prompt the response: "We believe in God. . . ." Furthermore, the proper confession of faith made at Mass is the Eucharistic prayer itself in which God is thanked and celebrated for all his works. As it is, the Creed too often becomes one more thing to be recited aloud, without having any particular connection with what comes before or after.

The same might be said of the general intercessions, or bidding prayers, though in fact Christians have from the

very beginning taken this opportunity at the end of the
Liturgy of the Word to make their petitions to God for
whatever was on their minds. It is not simply a way of
unloading an individual's private concerns onto God in a
public forum, however. It is rather an act of the community as a whole, commending to the Lord the world
which the community is sent to serve. God has put us here
together as a Christian community for a purpose: to work
with him and for him in the salvation of people from war
and suffering and hunger and loneliness and all the other
symptoms of sin. Prayer is an expression of our responsibility for our brothers and sisters under God: it is not a shift-
ing of responsibility. As Evelyn Underhill says, to offer
petitionary prayer is to offer ourselves to God, so that he
can use us if he chooses to answer that prayer. So a prayer
which simply shifted responsibility onto God would be
useless.

We should note, too, what it is we pray for. The
General Instruction on the Roman Missal suggests that
prayer should be offered for four types of intentions: [1]
for the needs of the worldwide Christian community, [2]
for civil authorities and for the needs of the whole world,
[3] for those oppressed by any kind of need, and [4] for the
local community. So we don't pray for ourselves — at least,
not in first place. Rather, our prayer represents a raising of
our eyes to the larger world of which we are a part and in
which we have a role to play: a role, namely, of bringing
the compassion and the healing of God himself to the
whole human family. Americans tend to be somewhat pro-
vincial, with little awareness of how others live or what
they suffer or how they think. So the bidding prayers
represent a call to be truly catholic in our interests and con-

cerns, and they must not be turned into an occasion for mentioning our personal concerns as if they alone counted. Rather, they give us a chance to pray for others, especially for those who cannot pray for themselves, for we have been ordained in baptism as priests for the whole human race.

III. Conclusion: Some General Principles

We can summarize the important principles governing the Liturgy of the Word in four brief comments:

1. The importance of the Word of God is that it is God himself speaking to us. The Liturgy of the Word is not a class in religious or moral truths, but a dialogue between God and his people, a dialogue carried out in reading and reflection, in attentive listening, and in the response of prayer.

2. This Word of God, recognized in our lives in the light of Scripture, is first taken to heart and then rises to our lips in the profession of faith, in the intercessory prayers, and, above all, in the Eucharist that follows.

3. The Introductory Rites, beginning with the entrance hymn and concluding with the prayer of the day, serve to prepare us to hear the Word of God by taking us as a scattered group of people and welding us into a prayerful, attentive community.

4. Our experience of the Liturgy of the Word should be that of being one people, gathered into one Body by the Lord, finding ourselves in the presence of the Father, who reveals himself to us anew and calls us to be his people and his witnesses in the world of our day.

DISCUSSION QUESTIONS

1. What problems, if any, do you and your fellow parishioners have with the Sunday readings? Are they audible throughout the church? Are they read intelligibly? Can you usually make sense of them? If not, why not?

2. What can be done to ease these difficulties?

3. What difference does it make to consider the readings as the Word *of* God and not just words *about* God?

4. What is your experience of the Introductory Rites? How can they help us to "celebrate these sacred mysteries"?

5. How can such elements as the entrance hymn, the celebrant's greeting, the other introductory rites, and the responsorial psalm help to make the Word of God more intelligible?

3   The Liturgy of the Eucharist

In the last chapter we spoke about the first two parts of the Mass: the Introductory Rites and the Liturgy of the Word. Now we turn to the second two parts: the Eucharistic Liturgy and the Concluding Rites.

I.   THE EUCHARISTIC LITURGY

Obviously it is not possible to deal adequately with every aspect of the Eucharist or to do justice to all that the believing community has discovered in this rich and wonderful rite in the course of two thousand years of celebrating it. Consequently, we shall concentrate here, as we did in speaking of the Liturgy of the Word, on those aspects which are important for those who are charged with planning the liturgy. In other words, we shall focus mainly on the structure of the rite, its different parts and how they relate to each other.

When Christ celebrated that Last Supper with his disciples on the night he was betrayed, he told them, "Do this in memory of me." But what was it that he was doing that we had to do in his memory? From all accounts he was celebrating a meal, a Jewish ritual meal. It was probably not a Passover meal in the strict sense, though some echoes of the Passover celebration have colored the Church's memory of that occasion and its understanding of what

Jesus was doing. But in any case, it was a meal into whose ritual Jesus inserted new meaning of his own, so that it became not just another celebration of the Exodus of old, but a celebration of the new deed of liberation that God was accomplishing in Jesus himself. This new meaning was attached not so much to the meal itself as to the ritual with which it began and with which it was concluded. For, we are told, when he came to table with his disciples, Jesus took bread, said a prayer blessing God, broke the bread and distributed it to them, saying, "This is my body which will be given up for you." And then, when the meal was over, he took a final cup of wine. Again he gave thanks to God, his Father, and passed the cup to his disciples, telling them, "Take this all of you and drink of it: this is the cup of my blood, the blood of a new and lasting covenant. It will be shed for you and for the whole human race for the remission of sins. Do this in memory of me."

It seems that in the early years of the Church, the Eucharistic memorial continued to be celebrated in the context of a full meal, with the breaking of bread at the beginning and the thanksgiving over the cup at the end. For various reasons, however, this did not last. The memorial meal shrank to the ritual which was specifically associated with Jesus: the taking of the bread and the cup, the offering of a prayer of blessing, the breaking of the bread, and the sharing of the bread and the cup by the followers of the Lord. In this way, the memory of the Lord was preserved as something living and vital right down to our own day. The form of the celebration continued to develop. It eventually moved out of the domestic setting in which it had been born and came to be celebrated by large congregations in public buildings. The common table came to be replaced by an altar in a roped-off area of the hall. The simple, almost informal ritual of the early days developed into an elaborate rite, accompanied by processions and music and chant. At a later stage, the evolution of the rite did not keep up with the changes in popular language, and it continued to be celebrated in Latin even when the people no longer understood it. Ordinary bread and wine brought by the people was replaced by special hosts. The rite became more and more a sacred act performed by a priest on behalf of a passive congregation, or even by a priest alone.

Yet, despite all that evolution, and despite the many different liturgical traditions which developed in East and West around the Eucharist, the basic pattern, however overgrown by other elements, remained the same. The basic pattern, inherited from the Lord himself and from the apostolic Church, consisted of four parts: for (a) the Lord took bread and wine; (b) he said the prayer of blessing; (c) he broke the bread; and (d) he gave the broken bread and the cup to his disciples. What is important for us to recognize is that this fourfold pattern is to be found in the Mass today — not just in the words of consecration, but in the shape of the Eucharistic liturgy as a whole. We take bread and wine: the Offertory. We say the prayer of thanksgiving to God: the Eucharistic Prayer. We break the bread, in preparation for Communion. We share in the one bread and the one cup, as from the hand of the Lord himself, in the Communion rite. So it is not just the Words of Institution, but the whole Eucharistic rite, beginning with the Offertory and concluding with the prayer after Communion, which is done "in memory of him."

It is also certain that in the early years of the Church's history the Eucharist was celebrated on its own, without

any reading of Scripture — though there was probably
some kind of prayerful conversation in the course of the
meal itself. Once the Eucharistic memorial was separated
from the context of a full meal, however, it was quickly
joined to a service of reading and prayer, giving us the
shape of the Mass as we have it today. This arrangement
was more than simply pragmatic. It has survived because it
has been found to be right. Thus the community of the
followers of Jesus gather in his name, share their memories
of the wonders of God in the Gospel and in the Old Testament, lift their hands in prayer and then, moved and
prompted by the Word of God they have heard, commit
themselves again to God in Christ in the ritual which Jesus
gave them on the night he surrendered his own life to God.

Thus the Eucharist is not just a sacred rite to be celebrated because of its good effects. It is rather an act of
remembering God and his Christ, and of remembering in
such a way that we are drawn to give ourselves anew to
God and to our neighbors, as Jesus on that first occasion
was committing himself to his Father for the sake of the
world he loved. Thus it is important in any celebration of
the Eucharist to allow the hearing of the Word of God to
be the motivation of our prayer and praise and sacrifice.
Otherwise there is the danger that it becomes another boring ritual: the Mass is the Mass is the Mass. On the contrary, every Mass is new and different. Every Mass is a
remembering of the Jesus who gave himself for us, but a
remembering which takes place in different contexts — in
different seasons of the liturgical year, at different stages of
our own life, in different historical and social circumstances, with different groups of people, on different occasions, in different places, and in response to different

readings and different "memories" of God. In this way, the Mass can always yield new insight, become a new occasion for encountering Christ, reveal new aspects of our relationship with him and new understanding of what Eucharist is, who Christ is and who we are.

Much more could usefully be said on this idea of the connectedness between the Eucharist and the Word, and on the newness of every Mass, but this much should put us on our guard against thinking that when we have said, "The Mass means this," or, "The Mass is that," we have said it all. The Mass is many things, for it is the point of encounter between God and us in Christ; and neither God, nor Christ, nor even ourselves can be summed up in a simple definition. But let us move on to the ritual of the Mass itself.

II. The Preparation of Gifts

The first thing Jesus did was take some bread and, later, a cup of wine. That's all: no elaborate ritual. He just picked them up to use them. And that is what the early Christians did, as far as we can tell. When the liturgy of the Word was over, they brought forward some bread and some wine and put them on the table. A simple thing to do, we may think, but we know how it is with special occasions: even simple things become significant. The bride and groom have a wedding cake to celebrate their marriage; but can it be sliced beforehand? Can just anyone cut it? It has to be cut to be eaten, and the cutting of itself is not that important, but it takes on significance because this is the first thing they do together as husband and wife. It becomes a ritual act, a symbol of their common life and of the way they want their life together to be enriching for others too.

So, similarly, the mere putting of bread and wine on the table became significant. Even today, men or women will talk of their struggle to support their families as a struggle to put bread on the table. But here is no ordinary table. It is the table prepared by God for his people in the person of his Son. As such it becomes a paradigm for all tables everywhere, making us recognize in all food and drink the fruit of the earth and the work of human hands: the gift of God and of his human co-workers. It makes us see that all human labor is a cooperative venture. We dig and plant, but God gives the growth. We transform the world by our technology, but God gives the raw materials and the skill. Even the laws of science are those that he himself has established in creation.

Besides that, there is something special about Christ choosing food and drink to be the symbols of his self-giving, because food and drink exist not for themselves but for other living creatures. They surrender their own existence to enter into the lives of others; we might say that food and drink sacrifice themselves so that others might live. A carrot exists not to be a carrot, but to be eaten to give life to other creatures. Bread does not exist for itself, but for the hungry. Wine is not made to be put on a shelf forever; it is made to be poured out and shared by friends as a symbol of their common life and common joy. That is how Jesus identified himself: under the forms of bread and wine, as the man who lived not for himself, but for others, that through his self-sacrifice others might live.

This is the point in the Mass when the collection is taken up — at the moment when the bread and wine are being placed on the table. Why? For many centuries it was not only bread and wine which were brought up. People brought corn and oil and eggs and cheese and spare clothing — whatever they had that they didn't need for themselves. It was the moment of redistributing the wealth of the community, so that no one grew fat while another starved, and no one kept coats in the wardrobe while others shivered in the cold. They could not celebrate the memory of Jesus' gift of himself without themselves being generous with one another. Some bread and wine was selected from all the gifts that had been handed in. This select portion was placed on the altar-table, while the rest of the gifts were put in large baskets to be taken out afterwards and distributed to the needy: the sick, the widows, the unemployed, those in prison, and so on. This was part of what they saw had to be done in obedience to Jesus' command, "Do this in memory of me." To remember Christ was not just to think about him: it was to live as he lived and to love as he loved, in very practical ways.

Today what we often refer to by its old name as "The Offertory" is properly called "The Preparation of the Gifts." By this we mean God's gifts to us and our gifts to God. But really we cannot give anything to God himself unless it be by way of giving to his people. We therefore need to restore the sense of the collection as a realistic redistribution of wealth. We need to know that it is going to be used for this purpose. While the maintenance of the church property and the support of parish programs are important, we should be careful not to let them absorb all our resources. In a parish, the Justice and Peace Committee or the St. Vincent de Paul Society should be responsible, as the deacons were of old, for supervising the distribution of the community's wealth.

This is the most important thing to be recognized about the Offertory or Preparation of the Gifts. For a while, in recent years, we used to bring up all sorts of goods, from school exercise books to miners' helmets, as symbols of our work. But that is ultimately unhelpful, an empty symbol — if only because those items were taken back again after the Mass and did not benefit anyone besides the donors themselves. That sort of thing has gone out of style by and large, but even now we should not make much of the Offertory procession unless we are sure that it has some serious connection with the meaning of the Eucharist.

In planning the Preparation of the Gifts, it is good to remember that it is basically a matter of putting the bread and wine for the Eucharist on the altar-table. On occasion it might make sense, in view of the readings that have preceded, or in view of the special occasion, to leave the altar bare up to this point and then to prepare for the Eucharist by covering the table with a cloth, bringing candles, and so forth. But what is really important is that the table be simple and uncluttered. Everyone should see the bread placed there with the cup — or cup and jugs — as the focus of the community's attention. It should not be obscured by a clutter of missals, missalettes, microphones and microphone wires, cruets, cloths, flowers, altar cards and what-have-you.

III.   THE EUCHARISTIC PRAYER

Having taken the bread, and later after he had taken the cup, Jesus said a blessing. In accordance with Jewish custom, he did not bless the bread and the cup, but he blessed God his Father *over* the bread and the cup. The

Jews have *berakoth* or blessings for every occasion. These are prayers of praise or acknowledgement, recognizing the presence and action of God in all the events of life. On solemn occasions, such as at a ritual meal, these short prayers are extended into a series of prayers of blessing. In them God's love of the world is acknowledged — his creation of the world and of food to sustain us, and then his mighty acts whereby he chose and delivered a people for himself. On the basis of the past, the Jews pray with confidence to God to complete his work on earth and bring his plan for the world to fulfillment.

It was this kind of prayer that Jesus offered at the Last Supper when he blessed his Father. No doubt Jesus would have improvised somewhat, to include in his praise and thanksgiving the new revelation of God's merciful love, which was taking place in his own life and death. And, no doubt, on the eve of his betrayal and crucifixion, Jesus prayed for God's will for the world to be done and for God to bring to completion the work he had begun in Jesus. In fact, it is precisely these ideas which we find in the great prayer of Jesus in St. John's account of the Last Supper.

It was from that prayer of Jesus, handed down and developed by the tradition of Christians celebrating the Eucharistic memorial for centuries, that our present Eucharistic Prayers have developed. The recitation of the Eucharistic Prayer, then, is the fulfillment of one part of Jesus' command to do this in memory of him: it is the blessing and praise of God the Father in memory of Jesus.

We do not know the exact words Jesus used in his prayer of blessing, so that over the course of time there has grown up an immense variety of Eucharistic Prayers. Yet what is common to them all, and presumably to the prayer of Jesus himself from whom they derive, is a certain basic pattern. They start off with a blessing or praising of God: "Father, all-powerful and ever-living God, we do well always and everywhere to give you thanks. . . ." Then, according to the occasion, different memories are evoked as motives for this thanksgiving: the creation of the world, the sending of his Son, the birth of Jesus, his life and work and above all his suffering, death and resurrection, and the sending of the Holy Spirit. We remind God and ourselves that we are doing this because Jesus himself told us to do it in his memory, and we ask God to send his Spirit upon us and upon our gifts that we may be drawn more and more into unity with him and with one another. We pray God to bring to fulfillment what he has already begun in history and in our lives. We look forward to the end of history when God's plan will be complete and when we shall be joined in one great, joyful community with all the dead, with Mary and all the saints, and with Christ himself as our head, so that through him and with him and in him God will have praise and thanksgiving from all his creation for ever and ever.

Again the pattern is very simple: it begins with what God has done in the past—in creation, in the Old Testament, and above all in his Son Jesus Christ. And it looks to the future, to the consummation and unification of all things in Christ, when all division will be overcome and all sorrow ended and every tear wiped away. And it situates the present moment in that context: this Sunday in June, this time of bereavement, this marriage, this period of war and suffering, or this time of joy and gladness. We pray for the Holy Spirit of God to enter anew into our history and into our lives through this celebration, so that God's work of salvation may be experienced now and, through our sanctified lives, be brought closer to its completion.

This is the overall pattern of the Eucharistic Prayer. Clearly, more could be said about it, but now our attention is drawn to the temporal dimension of the Prayer, for this is important for liturgical planning. With the variety of Prayers we have — not only four regular Eucharistic Prayers, but two other Prayers for reconciliation and three for children, plus sixty or so prefaces — it is up to us, when planning a liturgy, to select that Prayer or preface which most aptly fits the occasion of our celebration and the memories and promises of God evoked by the Liturgy of the Word. Most of the Eucharistic Prayers have exchangeable prefaces or introductory sections. We note, however, that the fourth Eucharistic Prayer and those specially designated for use at Masses of reconciliation and at children's Masses are not adaptable in that way. They are written as single prayers from beginning to end, and the variable prefaces will not match these Prayers.

We note, too, that the Eucharistic Prayer makes clear the character of the whole Eucharistic celebration as the celebration of Christ's sacrifice. It is an act of remembering before God the self-sacrifice of Jesus who, in submission to his Father and for love of us all, did not try to evade death, but let himself be crucified and killed rather than be unfaithful. Remembering the death of Jesus is not something that can be done simply by thinking about it. To remember Jesus is to live as he lived, to think as he thought, to act as he acted. To remember the death of Jesus is not just to be moved to tears by old memories, but to heed the words of Paul to the Philippians (2:5-8):

Have the same mind in you which was in Christ Jesus,
who, though he was in the form of God,
did not count equality with God a thing to be grasped,
but emptied himself, taking the form of a servant,
being born in the likeness of men.
And being found in human form
he humbled himself and became obedient unto death,
even death on a cross.

The purpose of celebrating the liturgy is not to give lip-service to God, but to glorify him as Jesus glorified him. We do this by transforming our lives under the influence of the Spirit of Jesus so that we become increasingly Christ-like in our total devotion to God and to the welfare of others. Jesus glorified his Father before the world by being totally given over to the Father's work in the world, no matter what the cost to himself. We celebrate the memory of Jesus in the Eucharistic sacrifice by offering our own lives together with Jesus for the life of the world. This we do, above all, in giving our assent to the Eucharistic Prayer and in the reception of Communion, as we shall see.

It should be clear from this that while the Mass is a sacrificial act its purpose is not simply to celebrate and represent the once-for-all sacrifice of Jesus, but to draw us sacrificially into the pattern of his self-offering so that we become increasingly conformed to the will of God, obedient even unto death. Thus the celebration of the Eucharist is inseparable from our conversion to a deeper life with God and to a profounder life of obedience. But what is being asked of us? That is what we discover in the circumstances of our lives as they are brought under the light of God's Word and as we entrust them to him in the celebration of the sacrifice. We tend naturally to think of ourselves as autonomous, making our own lives for ourselves and others. But the Liturgy of the Word reveals the deeper pattern of God's activity, and the Liturgy of the Eucharist calls us to surrender to that activity.

While this has important implications for our own spirituality, it also has significance for the planning of a liturgy, for it reveals the inseparable connection between Word and sacrament. We offer the sacrifice by partaking of the sacrament, but it is the Word of God in the Liturgy of the Word which calls and motivates and empowers us to do this. Thus the liturgy of the sacrament — whether it be the celebration of the Eucharist, or of baptism, or whatever — is always a response to the Word which has been proclaimed. As liturgy planners we want to be sensitive to that, to try to ensure as best we can that the message of the Word is echoed in the prayers and images of the sacrament. Thus the choice of a Eucharistic Prayer or of a particular preface is not arbitrary. Instead of simply using each of the four main Eucharistic Prayers once every four weeks, we should decide which of them, in the light of the Scripture readings, is most appropriate. The Word which we have taken to heart can then rise to our lips as prayer.

The acclamations during the Eucharistic Prayer are meant to help the congregation enter into and identify with the Prayer. The acclamations are the *Sanctus*, the memorial acclamation after the Institution Narrative, and the final *Amen*. These are devices, as it were, for engaging the assent and enthusiasm of the people, but they sometimes run the risk of seeming to chop the Eucharistic Prayer into three parts. We have to be sensitive to that, particularly in ensuring that the *Sanctus* and the other acclamations do not become so lengthy and elaborate that they take over altogether. It would be preferable to have more interventions and shorter ones, something along the lines of what has been provided in the Eucharistic Prayers for children, where the acclamation becomes a recurring refrain, rather than a kind of interlude in the Prayer itself. It is also helpful when a congregation has developed the custom of standing for the Eucharistic Prayer. Of course, kneeling is a good attitude for prayer, too, but it is a posture which suggests abasement and penance and, while there is a lot of room for that in Christian life, it is questionable whether it best expresses what we are about at Eucharist. At the Eucharist we are praying less in our own name than as the Body of Christ. We identify ourselves with the one whom the book of Revelation sees as slain yet standing before the throne of God, and there seems something appropriate in our adopting, even now, this posture of resurrection and victory and confidence as we proclaim the works of God and urge him to bring them to completion.

IV. THE BREAKING OF BREAD

The third thing Jesus did at the Last Supper was to break the bread which he had taken and over which he had offered blessing. Again, this was basically a functional gesture: for a loaf of bread to be shared among several people it had to be cut or broken. But the fact that there was only one loaf to be divided among all those present struck Christians as significant from the very beginning. St. Paul put it well to the Corinthians: "Because there is one bread, we who are many are one body, for we all partake of the one bread" (1 Cor 10:17). Indeed, this was primarily how early Christians saw the Eucharist: they called it "the breaking of bread." It was a sacrament of the new unity which God was establishing in the human family through the death of Jesus and the outpouring of the Spirit, a unity which embraced men and women, Jews and Gentiles, and ignored all the old historical enmities and all the accepted social and economic barriers between people.

For centuries, the actual way of celebrating Mass obscured this primary symbolism. The rise of individualism was accompanied by the development of private Masses and the introduction of individual hosts for those who wished to receive Communion. Yet the old action remained: the "fraction rite," where the priest broke his large host in two. Never mind that the rubrics called for him to eat both pieces himself! The symbol lay there, awaiting rediscovery. In the new Missal, the "fraction" once again becomes an important gesture. Although small individual hosts have not been banned — they are, after all, very convenient — still the sense of the rite now requires us to have large pieces of bread, or small loaves, which can be seen to be broken and shared among the multitude.

The breaking of bread, however, was not just a nice idea for the early Christians. It is a profound truth: a sign of the unity given us in Christ, a unity which triumphs over all human differences, prejudices and inequalities. A sacrament is not just an empty sign, an aesthetic symbol: it contains and requires what it signifies. The breaking of bread is a sacramental sign of the irrelevance of our divisions and classes. It *makes* them irrelevant. But we have to take that seriously in our own lives, which means living as if there were no classes, no racial differences, no social or economic barriers between people. It means dropping our grudges and our suspicions and our prejudices. For this reason, the actual breaking of bread is preceded by the Our Father and the exchange of peace.

The Our Father is the prayer Christ taught us, the prayer we have to learn to say wholeheartedly if we are to have part with him. It teaches us to speak of God as our common Father, thereby making it impossible to treat anyone as if he or she were not part of our family. It teaches us to pray for our daily bread — the bread, the support of life — that comes from God, the giver of life, of which the Eucharist is a symbol. But then it reverts to the theme of reconciliation and unity: "Forgive us our trespasses as we forgive those who trespass against us." Another way of putting this would be: accept us unconditionally, and we will try to do the same for one another. The meaningfulness of the breaking of bread depends upon our realization of our oneness under God and upon our willingness to actualize it in our relations with one another.

The same idea lies behind the exchange of peace. This is not simply a gesture of love or friendship. It is, more specifically, an act of reconciliation. In the eastern churches, it takes place at the Offertory because Jesus said:

> If you are offering your gift at the altar and there remember that your brother has something against you, leave your gift there before the altar and go; first be reconciled to your brother, and then come and offer your gift. (Matt 5:23-4)

Even in its present position before Communion in our rite, the meaning is the same. To eat of the one bread is to enter into communion, both with Christ and with one another in Christ. There is no union with Christ which can take place while excluding any other members of his Body. So the exchange of peace ought not to be a light interlude, but the final step before the actual breaking and sharing of the one bread which expresses our unity in Christ.

We can underline this by insisting on the fullness of the sacramental sign: a real breaking of bread, visible to all; and an end to the practice of distributing Communion from hosts reserved in a tabernacle.

The point is that Jesus did not leave us a message or a theology: he left us with something to do: "Do this. . . ." It is by doing it that we discover what he meant. We discover the meaning of the Eucharist by being obedient to his command to break bread together.

V. Eating & Drinking: The Communion Rite

The fourth thing Jesus did was to pass the bread and the cup to his disciples, telling them to take it, to eat and to drink. This corresponds to our Communion Rite.

We have various phrases for expressing what goes on here. We talk about "going to Communion," or "receiving Communion," or "administering" or "giving out Holy Communion." These phrases sound strange when we reflect on them. What does the word "Communion" mean? Some people talk about "communicating." But communications theory tells us that it takes two to communicate and they must both be involved, whereas "giving out Communion" suggests distributing something that people can take away with them. Perhaps we should talk about the "act of Communion," for Christ cannot enter into communion with us unless we communicate with him.

The restoration of the cup of his blood, as a sacramental sign in which all the faithful can now share, is particularly significant for helping us see what is involved in communion with Christ. On the one hand, wine has associations of joy and festivity, so that drinking from the cup is a sacramental anticipation of our participation in the banquet in the Kingdom of God. It looks forward to the joy of everlasting life with God and his saints, which the Scriptures so often describe in terms of a feast. But there is another, not unconnected, set of associations: the cup as cup of destiny and cup of suffering. In the agony of facing his imminent passion and death, Jesus prayed that, if it could be his Father's will, this "cup" might pass him by. When James and John asked for prominent places in the eternal Kingdom, Jesus asked them if they could drink of the cup that he himself would have to drink (Mark 10:38). All these associations come crowding back as we lift to our lips the cup of his blood, impressing upon us the fact that we are called to share in the likeness of his death if we are to have any share in the likeness of his resurrection (Rom 6:5).

Moreover, the meaning of the breaking of bread, as we have seen above, indicates that our communion with Christ is a communion with his Body, the community. It is not only that Christ is communicating himself to us but that we are communicating with him and with one another.

Interestingly enough, the term "Holy Communion" originally referred to what we would now call the Church community. In the Creed we still mention "the communion of saints," i.e., the community of holy people, the baptized. We believe in one, holy, catholic and apostolic

Church, which *is* the communion of saints. The Eucharist was then referred to as the sacrament of communion — the sign and sacrament of the common life we share in Christ. So St. Augustine comments that when the priest says, "The Body of Christ," and we say, "Amen," we are saying "Amen" to what we are. Long before it became popular with dieters and vegetarians, St. Leo the Great had coined the phrase, "You are what you eat," specifically in talking about the Eucharist. We are the Body of Christ: he the head, we the members, members of him and of one another.

This, too, is important for us to be aware of when we are planning liturgies. We have to find ways of celebrating the Communion Rite in such a way that people realize they are communicating with one another in Christ. To receive a piece of broken bread, instead of a little individual wafer, is one way. Drinking from a common cup is another. But we also have to do something with the Communion procession. Let me put the problem this way: how is going up to Communion a different kind of experience from standing in line at a check-out counter? One way to mark the difference, of course, is by careful selection of the music which accompanies the Communion Rite, and especially by using music which people can sing on the way to Communion. A song like "One Bread, One Body" says something different from "Jesus My Lord, My God, My All."

This is not to minimize the need for time for personal prayer and devotion. But the time for that is after the distribution is over. Then there should be a time for silence, a time for reflecting on the Communion of which we are part — one with others in Christ. This silent prayer is gathered together and summed up in the post-Communion prayer.

Note that the post-Communion prayer is the end of the Communion Rite, not the beginning or middle or end of the Concluding Rites. In many churches it marks the beginning of the end, or it even follows the notices and appeals and second collections. This is all wrong. The post-Communion prayer is just that: the community's prayer at the end of the Communion Rite.

VI. CONCLUDING RITES

With the post-Communion prayer, the Mass is essentially over. But we need some way of returning from the intensity of prayer and celebration to the ordinariness of our daily lives together. Just as at the beginning we need the Introductory Rites to get into the proper frame of mind, so we need some sort of conclusion to send us on our way. This is what the Concluding Rites provide. They consist of three things: [1] community business, [2] blessing, [3] dismissal and exit.

First, the community business. While the community is gathered here, this is a good opportunity to make announcements and deal with community business. One could imagine having a sort of parish meeting here after Mass. This would be the time for various representatives of parish groups to announce forthcoming activities, ask for volunteers, make the community aware of specific needs or problems. This is obviously the place where special financial appeals should be made, not after the Gospel. It is also the place where letters from the bishop should be read unless they take the form of a commentary on the Scriptures of the day, in which case they represent a homily by the bishop. While the appropriate person to give the homily will usually be the celebrant, at this point anyone can be allowed to get up and address the community. This is not preaching, but the community discussing its affairs.

When all that is over, the leader of the celebration greets the people anew and invokes God's blessing upon them as they return to their Christian lives in the larger world.

Finally, the order is given to disperse: to go forth as bearers of Christ's peace and to be faithful to him in serving the Father in the world. To the accompaniment of a suitable hymn or a musical piece, the ministers withdraw and the gathering disbands only to meet again to renew its identity and its commitment in another week. And so the work of God continues for the redemption of his world.

VII. CONCLUSION: SOME GENERAL PRINCIPLES

1. Planners must always bear in mind the fundamental fourfold pattern of the Eucharist: the Preparation of the Gifts, the great Prayer of Thanksgiving or Eucharistic Prayer, the Breaking of Bread, the Communion Rite.

2. Planners must always ask of each part, and of each component of each part: What is it for? What do the texts and gestures express? How does it fit in with what precedes and follows it? How can we best express its significance on this occasion?

DISCUSSION QUESTIONS

1. What did Jesus tell us to do in remembrance of him, and how is our present liturgy faithful to that command?

2. What is the role of the Holy Spirit in the Mass?

3. What considerations should be borne in mind in choosing hymns for the Preparation of the Gifts and for Communion? Select a hymn for each and show why it would be appropriate.

4. Do you think everyone should always "go to Communion"? Should we always be able to receive from the cup?

5. "The Church is a communion." Discuss.

6. What connections do you see between the celebration of the Eucharist and your life as a Christian in the world?

4 Planning the Liturgy

The first question to be asked about liturgical planning is not "how?" but "why?" Why should a liturgy have to be planned, and what do we think we are doing when we involve ourselves in liturgy planning?

For some years, following Vatican II, there was a lot of talk in Catholic circles about "experimental liturgies" as if, in reaction against the rigidity and immutability of the old rites, we felt it was incumbent upon us to re-invent the wheel every Sunday and never to do the same thing in the same way twice. At the present time, when those in Protestant churches which have never had much tradition of liturgical celebration are coming to appreciate the value of liturgy, they are talking a great deal about "worship experiences." Perhaps the common element in both is that well-worn cliché "having a meaningful experience." Obviously, no one of sound mind will keep on doing something that is utterly without meaning, but the basic question is whether the liturgy is something to which we have to give meaning, or whether it is something whose meaning we have continually to discover. The temptation for people dedicated to making liturgy meaningful is to think they know what the liturgy should mean and then to impose that meaning on the rites.

It is important to remember that we have inherited a liturgy: a series of traditional rites for the celebration of

Christian intiation, Eucharist, marriage, funerals, and so forth. Even in their revised form, the liturgical rites are very traditional, originating far away and long ago and developed through centuries of prayer and practice by successive generations of believers. Thus they are very old. But at the same time, and in a very real and important sense, they are very new. It is always the Mass that we celebrate, always the canonical Scriptures that we read. Yet every Mass is a new Mass, a unique event, and every reading of the Word of God comes alive as it is heard by this group of people, at this particular time, in this particular place, under these particular conditions.

Thus there is something intrinsically paradoxical about liturgy: a series of tensions which must not be relaxed. In addition to the tension between past and present, old and new, there are other tensions. Liturgy is a human event, subject to all the laws of group dynamics, communications theory, and so forth; at the same time it is a work of God on our behalf. It is an act of worship offered to God, and it is God's work among us. It is directed to God, yet it involves human interaction as the medium both of worship and of sanctification. It is essentially a community activity, yet it would be worthless if there were no personal engagement, no personal encounter with God.

As liturgy planners we must know clearly what we are about. We need a philosophy of liturgical planning. Everyone involved in liturgy has such a philosophy, of course. They have certain ideas of what they are doing, whether or not they are very clear or critical in understanding what they are doing. Hence problems often arise in parishes when different people have different expectations.

A philosophy of liturgical planning should have as its

major principle the recognition of the need to keep these polarities in tension: the divine and the human; the communal and the personal; the givenness and the newness; the upward movement of worship and the downward movement of sanctification; the encounter and union with Christ which is mediated by, but not totally identifiable with, encounter and union with one another in the community itself; the value of the liturgy for teaching people about God and the Christian life, and the role of liturgy as an actual encounter with God—an actual exercise of the Christian life; and so on.

It is no small task to keep these polarities in tension, but the need to do so can serve as a general guideline for thinking about how to plan a liturgy. There is no need to elaborate further on these tensions or polarities because they were discussed in previous chapters, but it must be emphasized that we will run into trouble if we start simply by asking what we are going to do and how we are going to do it. For this reason, it is an excellent idea for a parish liturgy planning committee to discuss what the Sunday Mass or the seasons of the liturgical year or the rites of baptism are about.

This is best not done by simple discussion, because that can lapse into simple argument and simple disagreement and simple deadlock. Perhaps it would be better to conduct this initial preparation of the planning group in three stages:[1]

---

1. The following suggestions on how to proceed in preparing people to serve on a liturgy planning team are colored, in part, by the method of adult education proposed by Thomas Groome in his book *Christian Religious Education* (New York: Harper & Row Pubs., Inc., 1980).

1)   At the first session, each member of the team should
be able to say openly, and without fear of being contra-
dicted or corrected, what going to Mass means to him or
her. When the whole group has had a chance to say what
their experience is and how that relates to what they
believe, then the question should be posed as to which different past experiences — of going to church, of family life,
of religious education — have given rise to their different
images and expectations of the Mass and what effect they
have on us. Note that there is no question here of evaluating these views.

2)   At a second session, someone should be called in who
can present, in outline form, the shape and meaning of the
Eucharist in the Scriptures and as it has developed from the
primitive Church to the revised liturgy of Vatican II,
especially looking at what people thought was the purpose
of the Mass in different ages of the Church.

3)   At a third session, prospective members of the planning committee should discuss what impact the previous
presentation has had on them, how they now evaluate
their previous viewpoints, and which understandings or
images of the liturgy seem to be most helpful in contemporary Christian life. On the basis of this sort of preparation, there would be a good chance of a liturgy committee
having a consensus on the nature of its service, even
though different members still represented different em-
phases in their understanding of the Mass.

I.   The Planning Team

Mention of a planning committee raises the question of
who should be on such a committee. In the first place, the

local clergy should be involved, for they are ordained to preside over the liturgical celebration. If they have been involved in planning it, they will be in a better position to lead it, especially in their introductory remarks and in their homily, both of which are crucial to the inner dynamic of a liturgical celebration. For this reason, it would be important for all the priests serving the parish to be involved in the initial sessions just described: not as experts, but as equal participants. Thereafter, the priest who is to preside at a particular liturgy should be part of the team planning that liturgy.

Lay involvement in the planning of the liturgy is essential, for the liturgy is an activity undertaken by the whole community, and the planning committee should reflect the composition of the community. That is, there should be one or two people who are not involved in either clerical or lay ministries, if only because the view from the sanctuary is not the same as the view from the pews! Obviously, the readers should be present or, where there is a large number of readers for the various Sunday Masses, then the coordinator of the readers. The parish choir-director and the coordinator of other lay ministries should be present as well. Ideally, perhaps, where there are several Masses on a Sunday, there should be a planning team for each Mass, composed of celebrant, ministers, music director. Often enough, though, there is only one planning committee, planning only one main liturgy. In this case, the coordinator of the readers and the director of music will have to report back to their respective constituencies on the way the planning committee envisaged the meaning of the Word of God for this parish, so that it can influence the way they read and the music they sing at all Masses. It is important, either way, that readers, musicians, and singers have a strong sense of what kind of celebration this is and what it is all about. So, for example, a choir practice might begin with a prayerful reading of the Scriptures for this liturgy. A brief introduction to each piece being rehearsed might indicate why it has been chosen and how it fits into the celebration, so that it can be executed appropriately and, indeed, prayerfully.

II. What is Liturgical Planning?

Liturgical planning, as we have already hinted, means anticipating the actual celebration and envisaging what it will be like. What are the new conditions under which this familiar ritual is going to be enacted? Who will be there? White, middle-class families? Aging working-class folk? Black youngsters from the inner city? Hispanic farm workers? Why are they there? What is happening in the life of the community? (Planners must be sensitive also to the clash of calendars: is it Pentecost or Memorial Day weekend? the Thirty-first Sunday in Ordinary Time, or the day after an election? the First Sunday of Advent, or the day a local factory closes and puts most people there out of work?) In short, what is the context in which the Word of God is proclaimed in this community at this time? What is on people's minds when the Scriptures are read this weekend? Not that everything must turn around that, but it is important in thinking of which images from the Scripture and the liturgy are likely to resonate with the congregation at this time.

The point is not to get gimmicky or "relevant," but to realize that the proclamation of the Scripture and the discipline of the liturgy shape our faith-consciousness and help us to recognize what God is saying and doing in the world of our times and how we are called to work with him and for him.

III. THE SEQUENCE OF THE PLANNING MEETING

There are various ways of setting about planning a liturgy and the following method is only one of them, but it has the advantage of being found to work.

1)   Start with the readings.

The dynamic of the liturgy is such that the newness of the sacramental liturgy consists in its being celebrated as a response to the Word of God proclaimed in a particular Liturgy of the Word. So we start with a prayerful reading of the Scriptures. Here we change the order of readings from that found at Mass and start with the Gospel. This is because the first reading (from the Old Testament, usually) is chosen to shed light on the Gospel. The Gospel is the main reading, the indispensable one, so we start with a prayerful reading of the Gospel, allowing time for the words to sink in and for the images in the reading to take hold. Then, after a pause, we go to the Old Testament reading and do the same, again letting the images take hold. Then we do the same with the responsorial psalm and finally with the middle reading, which may or may not fit in with the others.

The object here is not to "get the message," but to let the images surface. We tend to be too quick to seize the "message" — usually a moralistic one. Instead, it might be better simply to go around the group and let people say what images struck them in the readings. For example, instead of reading the Gospel about the widow of Naim and her son and saying this shows that Jesus will raise us from the dead, too, at the last day, we just stick with the series of images—loss, bereavement, mourning, despair, the encounter with an impressive man, a word of hope believed, the transformation of sadness to gladness—images which are reinforced by the first reading about Elijah and the widow who lost her son. Now we line those images up on the life and experience of this community today. Through that double lens, what do we see in our own life and times? What images from contemporary life do these images of God's action in the past evoke? Where do we see the hand of God and hear his voice today? In other words, what have we to celebrate?

Perhaps a whole series of different images can be drawn up by the readings of any Sunday. But which ones resonate with the experience of this community at this time? The Word of God, we said, comes to us in the situations and events of our own lives and our own times. The work of the planning committee is to anticipate that happening on Sunday and to "set the congregation up," as it were, to be struck with those images and recognize what the Lord is saying. This is why the readers have to be there: so they know what it is they are proclaiming. If *they* don't know, the people in the pews have little chance of hearing anything more than yet another reading from the same old book.

So the question arises, once the main images have been discovered: how can we present these readings in such a way that people who get to hear them only once in a large congregation, without time for preparation or reflec-

tion, can still get the point of each reading? Perhaps the
celebrant will shape his opening remarks to lead people
to look for meaning in the texts they are about to hear.
Perhaps each reader will say a helpful word before proclaiming the sacred text. (But let there be a clear distinction
between what the reader says and where the Scripture
reading begins.) Perhaps a dialogue reading will suggest
itself, or a visual image placed in the entrance to the church
or in the sanctuary.

By this time, the celebrant will have the basic materials
for his homily: he will at least have the images which will
dominate the celebration, and he will be able to play with
those images to see what they yield for the time when he
has to lead the people in prayer and in prayerful acceptance of the Word of God.

2) Go back to the Introductory Rites.

The purpose of the Introductory Rites is to form a
heterogeneous crowd of people into a prayerful and attentive community, prepared to hear the Word of the Lord.
The dominant images of the Scripture reading, those which
will resonate with this community, provide a guide in
planning how the liturgy is to get under way. What is the
mood? Joyful or somber, thankful or penitent, exuberant
or thoughtful? What is the motivation for this celebration?
It is easy to notice how liturgy comes alive when there is a
special occasion, like Christmas or a marriage or even a
funeral. Why? Because people know why they are there;
they have a reason for being there, and everyone knows
what it is. That really is important for good Sunday
liturgy: a sense of common purpose and a sense of occa-

sion. So the planning committee has itself to be clear about the motive and motifs of this celebration. Only then can they allow those motivations and motifs to find expression in the Introductory Rites: in the choice of an entrance song, in the celebrant's greeting and opening remarks, in the emphasis which is to be given (or not to be given) to the penitential rites and the *Gloria.* Nothing is more destructive of meaning than having one thing after another, in no obvious sequence and for no clear purpose. So the Introductory Rites are an extremely important part of the Mass. It would be good to read the section in the *General Instruction on the Roman Missal* which deals with them to understand how they can be used and what each part is meant to do.

The final part of the Introductory Rites is, of course, the collect or opening prayer. Since this is the culmination of all that leads up to it, it needs to be continuous with what has gone before. Unfortunately, the collects we have at the moment have not been chosen with any reference to the readings to follow and are consequently very general in tone. This is fine, insofar as it makes them usable under any circumstances. The problem is that what fits any situation at all does not fit any particular situation especially well. It might be a good idea for the celebrant, therefore, if not for the whole planning team, to look at the collect and see whether a word or two of amplification here or there might not enable it to express the prayer of the community better. For example, instead of simply saying

> God of wisdom and love,
> source of all good,
> send your Spirit
> to teach us your truth . . . (Sunday 10)

perhaps the terms "wisdom," "love," "teach us your truth" could be made more concrete in reference to the images which are coming up in the readings. Caution is necessary here because there is a danger that the community's prayer to God can too often be turned into an indirect way of instructing the community, but it is worth a carefully disciplined effort.

3) Consider the responses.

Finally, we go back to the end of the Liturgy of the Word and look at the provision the liturgy makes for the community to respond to what it has heard. Does the Creed, a rather lengthy profession of faith summarizing the whole work of God from creation to the parousia, offer a natural response to what has gone before? Or is it in danger of becoming a kind of routine interruption in the flow of the rite? Perhaps the shorter Apostles' Creed could best be used on a regular basis, and the longer Nicene Creed recited or sung on occasion when it seems appropriate. After all, it is the Apostles' Creed which is found in our baptismal liturgy, so that it serves here to reaffirm our baptismal identity as the People of God.

Then there are the intercessions. Again the search for relevance has sometimes led to a certain narrowing of perspectives here, but the ignoring of relevant issues in the world can end up making the intercessions a collection of spiritual clichés. The *General Instruction* suggests we widen our horizon, looking beyond our own immediate concerns and those of our community to become truly catholic in outlook. The order of intentions suggested is [1] the worldwide Christian community; [2] the international human family and those who shape its destiny; [3] those who are suffering; and [4] the needs of the local community. What is involved here is our sense of our baptismal priesthood, our responsibility to lift up our whole human family to God in prayer. The liturgy committee should keep an eye on these intercessions, but they will probably want to delegate the week-by-week preparation of them to one of their members. One cannot but be struck, however, by the way intercessory prayer has remained through the centuries as one of the stable elements of popular religious life. One thinks of the novenas, the offering of Mass stipends, the special devotions, and the special shrines where people could place their intentions for prayer. If the intercessions at Mass are to succeed in meeting this perennial need, we will have to provide a way for people to offer their own petitions. In a small group this can be done by allowing spontaneous prayer, but at a Sunday Mass that is hardly possible. Perhaps there should be a box at the back of the church where people could put the petitions for which they would like the community to pray. Someone could be deputed to sort through them and order them during the Liturgy of the Word,[2] so that they could be announced in groups at the intercessions: a group for the sick, a group for those with family worries, a group for those looking for work or for housing, and so on.

---

2. Although those who performed this service for the community would be prevented from hearing the readings, they would be participating in the Liturgy of the Word, just as do those who care for infants during the Liturgy of the Word at baptism (see *Rite of Baptism for Children*, no. 14). A situation in which some people would *never* hear the Word of God should, of course, be carefully avoided.

4)   *Attend to the Eucharistic Rites.*

Obviously, the greater part of the planning meeting will have to be dedicated to the Liturgy of the Word, partly because it is the Liturgy of the Word which largely determines the character of each celebration and partly because it is there that most of the options open to a planning committee are to be found. Still, it would be a mistake to pass over the Eucharistic liturgy itself, for the meaning of it depends largely upon its being understood as a response to the Word of God that has been proclaimed. What we want to avoid is the impression that the Word liturgy is over and now we are on to something entirely different.

Thus a quick decision can be made about which Eucharistic Prayer is most suitable for this occasion and, if it allows for a variable preface, which of the many prefaces in the missal best echoes the images and memories evoked in the Word liturgy. Similarly, we might want to ask how it can best be proclaimed. Should it be sung on this occasion? Which acclamation best fits the nature of the occasion?

The Offertory, or Preparation of the Gifts, is best kept simple most of the time. On occasion, however, it may be fitting to make more of the procession with the gifts — especially if there are newly baptized or newly confirmed people present, or people taking part in the Communion for the first time. For them to be involved in an Offertory procession would help to underline the connection between offering and receiving. On occasion, too, especially if the image of the meal is one that has assumed a large role in the liturgy, the Preparation of the Gifts might include a preparation of the altar-table, with the spreading of the cloth and the bringing of flowers and candles.

Here, as in everything liturgical, the accent must be on authenticity. One of the major contributions of liturgy committees is to keep our parish worship honest. Let us have bread that is bread and can be broken, good wine, real wax candles, real table cloths, tasteful vestments, and honest-looking vessels. Let us also make a vow to expel from our churches whatever is shoddy and phony: whether they be plastic flowers or tin chalices or grubby altar cloths. Let us make war, too, on clutter, so that the basic symbols — the altar, the bread and wine, the president's chair, the book of the Scriptures — can stand out and speak for themselves. Vatican II demanded a reform of the rites in the direction of what it called "noble simplicity." Let us not go back on that with an unholy clutter of banners, posters, odds and ends of sanctuary furniture, bits of paper, and wires all over the place.

The Communion Rite is not something that has to be planned anew every weekend, but it is something that needs serious thought in the early days of a planning committee's life. There is the question, first of all, of making arrangement for enough ministers of bread and cup so that all can receive unhurriedly and with reverence. There are the physical arrangements to be attended to which can facilitate that. But in the long-term we should be thinking about how this procession to Communion can become a community act, an eating and drinking together in affirmation of our common life in Christ. Too often it is simply a matter of lining up and awaiting one's turn. How can we give expression to the horizontal dimension of Communion as communion with one another in Christ? Of course, preaching and catechesis can help, but we also need to think about the kind of music we sing. Often, for practical reasons, Communion is distributed in silence and then, as soon as the last person has received, the Communion hymn begins. It should be exactly the other way around. We should be singing as we share together the Body and Blood of the Lord. "Happy are those who are called to his supper," says the priest. Here the liturgy is alluding to the book of Revelation (19:9), where the angel says those words, commenting upon what John describes as a "great multitude" which he heard rather than saw! "Then I heard what seemed to be the voice of a great multitude, like the sound of many waters and like the sound of mighty thunderpeals. . . ." The sound of the People of God coming to take part in the wedding feast of the Lamb—that is what going to Communion should be like: the great and joyful feast in the Kingdom of God. And then, afterwards, silence. Silence to let it sink in. Silence to meditate upon the vision we have been given and to realize we are as yet far from it. Silence in which to pray for the coming of that Kingdom. It is out of that silence that the final prayer is offered in the name of the community: the post-Communion prayer.

5) Finish with the Concluding Rites.

With that, the Mass proper is over. But there is time before the community disperses to make announcements and to bring up matters of community business. It is the time, as suggested earlier, for reading pastoral letters, discussing finances, appealing for money, asking for volunteers, taking votes, or whatever else a lively Christian community might be concerned with. It concludes with the blessing and dismissal of the people, and perhaps with a hymn which, once again, recalls the images and symbols which have sustained the community throughout this celebration.

This reference to the Concluding Rites and to the wider activities of the community prompts some final reflections on the relation of the liturgy planning group to the rest of the parish.

IV. LITURGY PLANNING AND PARISH LIFE

Active participation in the liturgy was one of the battle cries of the liturgical movement and one of the guiding principles of the liturgical reform. It is rooted in the fact that God does not choose and save individuals as such, but that he has created and is creating a people for himself, to witness as a community in the midst of a divided and antagonistic world. It was because the old Latin liturgy did not adequately express that, although it was full of vestiges of such awareness, that it had to be revised. The revision of texts and the promulgation of new rubrics was a comparatively simple matter. It is quite a different matter — and a far more difficult one, we are discovering — to develop the corresponding attitudes and acquire a sense of ourselves as a people.

Until that does happen, however, the liturgy will never quite come alive. Until active participation in the liturgy becomes simply one manifestation of active participation in the common life of the People of God, it will be done by rote and without conviction. Likewise, Church leaders who promote active participation of the faithful in the liturgy, but effectively bar the parishioners from having any voice in how the community is run, are engaged in promoting contradictory policies.

The continuity between liturgy and life is not something each of us can simply forge for ourselves within the privacy of our own hearts and intellects. It has to find visible expression in our common life and work. It has to find expression, not least, in the structures of the parish itself. This brings us to our final question about liturgy planning: how does it relate to other parish activities?

Let us make here a distinction which is widely made with some success in parishes throughout the country, between a liturgy planning team and a liturgy committee. The role of the liturgy planning team is obvious: we have been describing it. It is to prepare the liturgies each week and for the major feasts and seasons. In a large parish, it would be advisable to have different planning teams for the different liturgies, but they would all be answerable to the liturgy committee of the parish. The role of the liturgy committee would be to evaluate liturgical practice, but particularly to serve as a liaison between liturgical celebrations and other related areas of parish life. One good example of this is the Liturgy and Spirituality Committee being set up in a parish near Notre Dame University. Such a committee would be responsible for such things as assessing the needs of the parish community, providing parish retreats, missions, days of recollection for different groups, and so on. They might also attend to such questions as how the parish is going to celebrate Lent. They could sound out the people, offer proposals, make arrangements. They might find a dearth of spiritual reading, a desire for prayer groups, a need for counselling and spiritual direction, and they would have to think of how these needs could be met. Thus the liturgy is seen to be more than a Sunday morning ritual: it is the common prayer of the community and, as such, it must both flow over into people's personal and social lives, and also feed off the day-to-day living of the Christian life.

But such a liturgy commission would also need to be in close contact with two other areas of parish life: education and what is now often called "justice and peace."

The connection with education is obvious. Much parish education takes the form of preparing people for the sacraments: preparing parents for the baptism of their children, preparing children for confirmation and first Communion, preparing people for marriage, preparing converts for reception into the Church. But the model of Christian formation offered us today by the *Rite of Christian Initiation of Adults* makes it impossible to continue on the supposition that first there is the instruction, then there is the liturgy. The stress today is on formation in the Christian life, a formation in which different liturgical celebrations are stepping stones or, better, markers which actually shape and direct the formation process. This would take us into another whole area of discussion, the role of liturgy in Christian formation, but let it suffice now to draw attention to it.

The other area of contact ought to be that of justice and peace, i.e., contact with those people in the parish who are concerned with the community's contribution to society, whether in terms of help to the poor and needy, or in terms of evaluating local, national and international political issues and striving to contribute to the political process. As we become increasingly formed by the liturgy and the Scriptures, it will become more and more difficult for us not to raise questions about our responsibility for the larger world. Praying for it is the first step, not the last. The celebration of the liturgy brings us week by week to encounter a God who has made himself a reputation as the lover of the poor, the liberator of the oppressed, and the vindicator of those who are victims of injustice. We shall increasingly find that as we take the liturgy more seriously, people will become increasingly concerned about social questions. How can we go on with the liturgical breaking of bread without sharing our wealth? How can we celebrate God's liberating work in Jesus Christ without being conscious of the millions of our fellow human beings for whom that liberation is so far from being a fact of their experience? It is interesting that many of the people who first became involved in liturgical reform in Europe and in the United States were what we would call today "social activists." If the liturgy did it for them, maybe it will do it for us. Certainly there should be representation of the justice and peace people on the liturgy committee, and the liturgy and spiritual life people should be represented on the parish social action committee.[3] Otherwise the two areas of Christian life in the parish might never meet: they would remain unintegrated instead of each helping the other to hear the Gospel.

The work of all committees and planning groups within the structure of parish life must be kept in perspective. In

---

3. For a more extensive treatment of this subject, *see* Mark Searle, ed., *Liturgy and Social Justice* (Collegeville, Minn.: The Liturgical Press, 1980). The authors address the theological linkage between social ministry and liturgical life in four essays: "Serving the Lord with Justice," "Preaching the Just Word," "The Sacrifice of Thanksgiving and Social Justice," and "Symbols of Abundance, Symbols of Need."

the end it is the role of the pastoral leader, the priest, not to run everything himself, but to keep different areas of activity in touch with one another and to coordinate the various gifts and insights of the People of God entrusted to his care.

V. CONCLUSION: SOME GENERAL PRINCIPLES

1. It is a good idea for people involved in liturgy planning first to sit down and reflect on what they are about.

2. The actual planning team should include all those exercising ministries in the actual celebration being planned, plus representatives from the congregation.

3. The suggested procedure for planning a liturgy starts with the Liturgy of the Word, and in particular with the Gospel, goes back to the Introductory Rites, and then forward to the Eucharistic liturgy.

4. The same principles would apply to planning specific liturgies, such as the Holy Week rites or the celebration of baptism, as well as liturgies for specific groups, such as children or the elderly, for example.

5. It is a good idea to have some way of connecting the planning and the celebration of the liturgy with other areas of community life, so that the liturgy does not become an end in itself, but both reflects and shapes the larger life of the parish.

DISCUSSION QUESTIONS

1. Discuss the order of priority to be given to the following values: high quality (of music, reading, preaching, etc.); prayerfulness; congregational involvement; reverence; variety; retaining traditional practices; following the rubrics; solemnity; homeliness; relaxed atmosphere.

2. Discuss why your group has given priority to some values, while another group of Christians might give priority to a different set of values. (Or, if you cannot come to consensus, try to see why some of you choose one set of values and the rest of you another: what does it say about *you?*)

3. Given your parish, should you have a liturgy committee and a planning team? How are responsibilities to be delineated between the two? Who should be invited to serve on each?

4. In the light of previous discussions, draw up a form of procedure for liturgy planning, provisionally allotting to each step an amount of time within the total timeframe of the planning session.

5. Discuss the advantages of planning individual celebrations before taking on the task of planning a whole liturgical season or year.

THE AUTHOR

DR. MARK SEARLE *was born in Bristol, England, in 1941. After his early education in England he studied in Rome, where he earned a licentiate in sacred theology. In 1969 he earned both a diploma in liturgical studies and a doctorate in theology in Trier, Germany.*

Dr. Searle is associate director of the Notre Dame Center for Pastoral Liturgy and assistant professor of theology at the University of Notre Dame, Notre Dame, Indiana. He is editor of the review Assembly *and serves as a consultant to the International Committee on English in the Liturgy. He has led workshops and lectured extensively in England and the United States.*

Included among his published works are cassette tapes for National Catholic Reporter *and numerous articles in* Assembly, Worship, The Way, Life and Worship, Christian Celebration, *and* Liturgy.

Dr. Searle is the author of Christening: The Making of Christians *and contributing editor of* Liturgy *and* Social Justice, *both published in 1980 by The Liturgical Press.*